Some basic expressions

Yes.	네.	ne
No.	아뇨.	a·nyo
Please.	어서.	ŏ·sŏ
Thank you.	고맙습니다.	ko·map·sŭm·ni·da
Thank you very much.	대단히 고맙습니다.	tae·dan·hi ko·map·sŭm·ni·da
That's all right.	천만에요.	ch'ŏn·ma·ne·yo

Greetings

Good morning.	안녕하십니까 ?	an·nyŏng·ha·shim·ni·ka
Good afternoon.	안녕하십니까 ?	an·nyŏng·ha·shim·ni·ka
Good evening.	안녕하십니까 ?	an·nyŏng·ha·shim·ni·ka
Good night.	안녕히 주무세요.	an·nyŏng·hi chu·mu·se·yo
Good-bye. (leaving)	안녕히 가세요.	an·nyŏng·hi ka·se·yo
Good-bye. (staying)	안녕히 계세요.	an·nyŏng·hi kye·se·yo
See you later.	또 뵙겠읍니다.	to poep·ke·ssŭm·ni·da
This is Mr. . . .	이분은 …씨입니다.	i·bu·nŭn . . . ssi·im·ni·da
This is Mrs. . . .	이분은 …부인입니다.	i·bu·nŭn . . . pu·in·im·ni·da
This is Miss . . .	이분은 …양입니다.	i·bu·nŭn . . . yang·im·ni·da

9

I'm very pleased to meet you.	만나서 반갑습니다.	man·na·sŏ pan·gap·sŭm·ni·da
How are you ?	별고 없으십니까 ?	pyŏl·go ŏp·sŭ·shim·ni·ka
Very well, thank you.	네, 덕분에.	ne tŏk·pu·ne
And you ?	당신은요 ?	tang·shin·ŭn·yo
Fine.	잘 지냅니다.	chal chi·naem·ni·da
Excuse me.	실례합니다.	shil·lye·ham·ni·da

Questions

Where ?	어디 ?	ŏ·di
Where is . . . ?	…은 어디입니까 ?	. . . ŭn ŏ·di·im·ni·ka
Where are . . . ?	…은 어디입니까 ?	. . . ŭn ŏ·di·im·ni·ka
When ?	언제 ?	ŏn·je
What ?	무엇 ?	mu·ŏt
How ?	어떻게 ?	ŏ·tŏ·ke
How much ?	얼마 ?	ŏl·ma
How many ?	몇개 ?	myŏt·kae
Who ?	누구 ?	nu·gu
Why ?	왜 ?	we
Which ?	어느 쪽 ?	ŏ·nŭ·chok
What do you call this ?	이것은 무엇이라고 합니까 ?	i·gŏ·sŭn mu·ŏ·shi·ra·go ham·ni·ka
What do you call that ?	저것은 무엇이라고 합니까 ?	chŏ·gŏ·sŭn mu·ŏ·shi·ra·go ham·ni·ka
What does this mean ?	이것은 무슨 뜻입니까 ?	i·gŏ·sŭn mu·sŭn tŭ·shim·ni·ka
What does that mean ?	저것은 무슨 뜻입니까 ?	chŏ·gŏ·sŭn mu·sŭn tŭ·shim·ni·ka

Do you speak . . . ?

Do you speak English ?	영어를 할 줄 아십니까 ?	yŏng·ŏ·rŭl hal·chul a·shim·ni·ka
Do you speak German ?	독일어를 할 줄 아십니까 ?	to·gil·ŏ·rŭl hal·chul a·shim·ni·ka
Do you speak French ?	불어를 할 줄 아십니까 ?	pu·rŏ·rŭl hal·chul a·shim·ni·ka
Do you speak Spanish ?	서반아어를 할 줄 아십니까 ?	sŏ·ba·na·ŏ·rŭl hal·chul a·shim·ni·ka
Do you speak Italian ?	이태리어를 할 줄 아십니까 ?	i·t'ae·ri·ŏ·rŭl hal·chul a·shim·ni·ka
Could you speak more slowly, please ?	좀 더 천천히 말해 주시겠어요 ?	chom tŏ ch'ŏn·ch'ŏn·hi mal·hae chu·shi·ge·ssŏ·yo
Please point to the phrase in the book.	이 책에서 그 말을 가리켜 주세요.	i ch'ae·ge·sŏ kŭ ma·rŭl ka·ri·kyŏ chu·se·yo
Just a minute. I'll see if I can find it in this book.	잠깐 기다려 주세요. 이 책에 그 말이 있는지 찾아볼 테니까요.	cham·kan ki·da·ryŏ chu·se·yo. i ch'ae·ge kŭ ma·ri in·nŭn·ji ch'a·ja·bol t'e·ni·ka·yo
I understand.	알겠읍니다.	al·ge·ssŭm·ni·da
I don't understand.	모르겠읍니다.	mo·rŭ·ge·ssŭm·ni·da

Can . . . ?

Can I have . . . ?	…을 주시겠읍니까 ?	. . . ŭl chu·shi·ge·ssŭm·ni·ka
Can we have . . . ?	…을 주시겠읍니까 ?	. . . ŭl chu·shi·ge·ssŭm·ni·ka
Can you show me . . . ?	…을 보여 주시겠읍니까 ?	. . . ŭl po·yŏ chu·shi·ge·ssŭm·ni·ka
Can you tell me . . . ?	…을 가르쳐 주시겠읍니까 ?	. . . ŭl ka·rŭ·ch'yŏ chu·shi·ge·ssŭm·ni·ka
Can you help me, please ?	도와 주시겠읍니까 ?	to·wa chu·shi·ge·ssŭm·ni·ka

Wanting

I'd like ...	…하고 싶은데요.	... ha·go shi·p'ŭn·de·yo
We'd like ...	…하고 싶은데요.	... ha·go shi·p'ŭn·de·yo
Please give me ...	…을 주세요.	... ŭl chu·se·yo
Give it to me, please.	그것을 주세요.	kŭ·gŏ·sŭl chu·se·yo
Please bring me ...	…을 갖다 주세요.	... ŭl kat·ta chu·se·yo
Bring it to me, please.	그것을 갖다 주세요.	kŭ·gŏ·sŭl kat·ta chu·se·yo
I'm hungry.	배가 고픕니다.	pae·ga ko·p'ŭm·ni·da
I'm thirsty.	목이 마릅니다.	mo·gi ma·rŭm·ni·da
I'm tired.	피곤합니다.	p'i·gon·ham·ni·da
I'm lost.	길을 잃었읍니다.	ki·rŭl i·rŏ·ssŭm·ni·da
It's important.	그것은 중요합니다.	kŭ·gŏ·sŭn chung·yo·ham·ni·da
It's urgent.	급합니다.	kŭp·ham·ni·da
Hurry up !	서두르세요!	sŏ·du·rŭ·se·yo

It is/There is ...

It is/It's ...	…입니다.	... im·ni·da
Is it ...?	…입니까?	... im·ni·ka
It isn't ...	…이 아닙니다.	... i a·nim·ni·da
There is/There are ...	…이 있어요.	... i i·ssŏ·yo
Is there/Are there ...?	…이 있읍니까?	... i i·ssŭm·ni·ka
There isn't/There aren't ...	…은 없읍니다.	... ŭn ŏp·sŭm·ni·da
There isn't any/ There aren't any.	전혀 없읍니다.	chŏn·hyŏ ŏp·sŭm·ni·da

A few common words

big/small	큰/작은	k'ŭn/cha·gŭn
quick/slow	빠른/느린	pa·rŭn/nŭ·rin
early/late	이른/늦은	i·rŭn/nŭ·jŭn
cheap/expensive	싼/비싼	ssan/pi·ssan
near/far	가까운/먼	ka·ka·un/mŏn
hot/cold	더운/찬	dŏ·un/ch'an
full/empty	가득한/빈	ka·dŭk·han/pin
easy/difficult	쉬운/어려운	swi·un/ŏ·ryŏ·un
heavy/light	무거운/가벼운	mu·gŏ·un/ka·byŏ·un
open/shut	열린/닫힌	yŏl·lin/ta·ch'in
right/wrong	맞는/틀리는	man·nŭn/t'ŭl·li·nŭn
old/new	낡은/새로운	nal·gŭn/sae·ro·un
old/young	늙은/젊은	nŭl·gŭn/chŏl·mŭn
beautiful/ugly	예쁜/미운	ye·pŭn/mi·un
good/bad	좋은/나쁜	cho·ŭn/na·pŭn
better/worse	더 좋은/더 나쁜	tŏ cho·ŭn/tŏ na·pŭn

A few prepositions and some more useful words

at	에	e
on	위에	wi·e
in	안에	a·ne
to	으로	ŭ·ro
from	에서	e·sŏ
inside	안으로	a·nŭ·ro
outside	밖으로	pa·kŭ·ro
up	위로	wi·ro
down	아래로	a·rae·ro

before	전에	chŏ·ne
after	후에	hu·e
with	과 (와)	kwa(wa)
without	없이	ŏp·si
through	을 통해서	ŭl t'ong·hae·sŏ
towards	을 향해서	ŭl hyang·hae·sŏ
until	까지	ka·ji
during	동안	tong·an
and	과 (와)	kwa(wa)
or	또는	to·nŭn
not	아닌	a·nin
nothing	아무것도 없는	a·mu·gŏt·to ŏm·nŭn
none	하나도 없는	ha·na·do ŏm·nŭn
very	대단히	tae·dan·hi
also	도 역시	to yŏk·shi
soon	곧	kot
perhaps	아마	a·ma
here	여기	yŏ·gi
there	거기	kŏ·gi
now	지금	chi·gŭm
then	그때	kŭ·tae

A very basic grammar

Explaining the basic principles of such an intricate and subtle language as Korean is not an easy matter. The difference between English and Korean is nothing like the difference between, say, French and English. The pattern we are used to, that of differences in conjugations and declensions, vocabulary and idioms, is one that is limited to our group of Western languages. As soon as one sets out to compare English with an Oriental language, the difference is much more profound. Moreover, Korean has the particularity of being practically unrelated even to any other Oriental language.

Generally speaking, a foreign language not only implies different words and sentence constructions, but also a different way of thinking and reasoning. This is all the more true for Korean. The country, the people, their customs and above all their language have been almost totally isolated for over 2000 years. The result is a totally different way of experiencing life.

Korean has a limited affinity with Chinese: they are related in writing and, to a certain extent, in vocabulary. The Koreans have adopted a great number of Chinese words and characters. These often have a polite, scientific or cultural bearing, in the same way as words of French (Latin) origin in English generally have a more lofty meaning than those of Anglo-Saxon origin. They are not normally those used in everyday language by the man in the street. Also, Korean is undergoing steady change and is developing as time goes on. Words disappear and new ones are picked up, just as the English spoken today is no longer that of Shakespeare's day.

Korean has a certain number of dialects; someone from the north of the country may be incapable of understanding a man from the south. However, when they get together they will generally make themselves understood by using the dialect of Seoul which is accepted as being the leading version of Korean.

A sentence in the making

The few grammatical notes below do not account for the psychology of Korean speech. You'll just have to keep in mind that it is virtually inconceivable to substitute for or translate a Korean phrase by an English counterpart. Here we are only concerned with the grammatical structure, the architecture of a Korean sentence.

The basic word order in Korean is subject — object — verb. This is a rather rigid rule: the verb always comes last in a sentence. Subordinate clauses always precede the main clause. Here's an example to illustrate those two facts. Where a speaker of English would say:

My wife wore a new dress when she came home.

a speaker of Korean would turn the parts of speech around and say:

My wife home came when, she a new dress wore.

Also, English tends to stress syllables within words and words within phrases. In our example, the words "wife," "dress" and "home" would probably carry more emphasis than the others. In Korean, however, stress is highly regular, all syllables and words are pronounced with almost equal force in a staccato way.

Nouns and adjectives

Korean nouns have no articles. Plurals do not exist either. Thus, the word **chaek** may mean book, the book, a book, books or the books. All nouns have one single form which does not change according to the noun's role in the sentence.

Korean adjectives, in turn, are also very different from their English counterparts. They have tenses and moods as if they were verbs. The true Korean adjective is an adjective with a sense of "to be" attached to it. An improvised rendition of "a new dress" in Korean could be "a new-being dress." The past tense of these adjectives is formed by replacing **da** with **atta** or **ŏtta**.

talda	sweet	**hŭrida**	unclear
talatta	"was sweet"	**hŭriŏtta**	"was unclear"

There are a certain number of adjectives which are formed differently: these are of Chinese origin. Bringing our Korean phrase up to date, we would say:

My wife home came when, she new-being dress wore.

Verbs

There is at least one field where Korean is much simpler than English: verbs. The Korean verb has only three tenses—present, past and future. However, this simplicity is largely offset by the existence of numerous polite forms. These are basically the result of the sharply-defined social strata in Korea which gave birth to numerous graduations in polite speech. The way our speaker feels about the dress his wife wore, and above all the person he is speaking to, will define the grade of politeness of the verb form he'll choose. They can hardly be expressed in English. Here's an example:

mŏkta	to eat	**mashida**	to drink
mŏksŭmnida	to eat (polite)	**mashimnida**	to drink (polite)

Apart from politeness, a great number of other ways of feeling, moods and opinions are expressed through a complex web of verb forms.

And there is yet another difference. The verbs, apart from having only three tenses, have no special form to indicate person or number. On top of that, personal pronouns are usually omitted. They, too, are understood from the context, and the Koreans feel that they're unnecessary.

What's now left of our sentence ? It has started taking the shape of a Korean sentence — pared down to its essentials. But we're not there yet.

Particles

Subject and direct object are not understood from the word order as in English. When a noun is used as a subject, either the particle **i** or **ga** or the particle **nǔn** or **ǔn** is added after it to indicate this; a noun used as a direct object takes the postposition **rǔl** or **ǔl**. In fact, particles are to Korean what word order and prepositions are to English. That is also true of questions. These are not formed by inversion of verb and subject, but usually the last particle **da** in the declarative sentence is changed to **ka**. Sometimes they are formed only by rising intonation, especially in familiar speech.

My wife·ga home came when, my wife·nǔn new-being dress·ǔl wore.

By now you must be curious as to how a real Korean would say that. Here it is:

아내가 집에 돌아왔을 때, 아내는 새옷을 입고 있었읍니다.
a·nae·ga chib·e to·ra·wat·sǔl·tae, a·nae·nǔn sae·os·ǔl ip·ko i·ssǒ·ssǔm·ni·da

If you have a close look at the sentence and compare the Korean characters with the transliteration and our English "translation", you'll see how it illustrates the rules explained above.

Those characters

It is beyond the scope of this book to go into a detailed explanation of how Korean is written; but the following concise description should provide a basis which may help you to decipher some signs and put you on the right track. Traditionally, Korean is written from top to bottom, starting in the upper *right*-hand corner. But it's also written horizontally and from left to right (as in this book).

Han·ja

Korean has taken over characters and vocabulary from Chinese. These Chinese characters are called *Han·ja*. The Korean government has approved a basic list of 1,800 of them, but there are many more. One dictionary even gives some 50,000! *Han·ja* are symbols for concepts: 1 word = 1 character, as opposed to *Han·gŭl*, which represent phonemes or speech sounds. *Han·ja* characters may consist of as many as 33 different strokes, but many of them have been simplified since World war II.

Han·gŭl

The unique Korean alphabet, *Han·gŭl*, was devised after many years of study by King Sejong and his scholars, and introduced in 1446 during his reign. It originally consisted of 28 characters. There are now 24 *Han·gŭl* characters. These are used for writing native Korean words. Before *Han·gŭl* was devised, Chinese characters were used. Chinese characters, however, were very difficult to learn and quite different from the Korean language, so most common people had to remain illiterate. But

Han·gŭl can be learned overnight. Koreans are very proud of *Han·gŭl* and King Sejong is highly respected as a national ero. October 9th is celebrated as *Han·gŭl* Day in Korea.

Korean consonants and vowels

In the Korean alphabet, basically, one consonant and one vowel combine to form one syllable. At the end of a syllable, though, consonants may be added. Though no more than one consonant may be used at the beginning of a syllable, two consonants may be added at the end of a syllable. When the letter "ㅇ" precedes a vowel at the beginning of a syllable it is not sounded, but when it is added at the end of a syllable, it is similar to "ng" in sound.

Vowels

아	야	어	여	오	요	우	유	으	이
a	ya	ŏ	yŏ	o	yo	u	yu	ŭ	i

Consonants

ㄱ	ㄴ	ㄷ	ㄹ	ㅁ	ㅂ	ㅅ	ㅇ	ㅈ	ㅊ
k	n	t	r, l	m	p	s	-, ng	ch	ch'

ㅋ	ㅌ	ㅍ	ㅎ						
k'	t'	p'	h						

Basic consonants **k, t, p,** and **ch** are pronounced as **g, d, b,** and **j,** respectively, when occurring in the middle of a syllable. The letter ㄹ is sounded like **r** when it comes at the beginning of a syllable, and like **l** at the end.

Quick reference page

Please.	부탁합니다.	pu·t'ak·ham·ni·da
Thank you.	고맙습니다.	ko·map·sŭm·ni·da
Yes/No.	네/아뇨.	ne/a·nyo
Excuse me.	실례합니다.	shil·lye·ham·ni·da
Waiter, please.	웨이터, 잠깐만.	we·i·t'ŏ, cham·kan·man
How much is that?	얼맙니까?	ŏl·mam·ni·ka
Where are the toilets?	화장실이 어딥니까?	hwa·jang·shi·ri ŏ·dim·ni·ka

화장실 (hwa·jang·shil)	Toilets
남자용 (nam·ja·yong)	여자용 (yŏ·ja·yong)

Could you tell me . . . ?	…을 가르쳐 주시겠어 요?	. . . ŭl ka·rŭ·ch'ŏ chu·shi·ge·ssŏ·yo
where/when/why	어디/언제/왜	ŏ·di/ŏn·je/we
Help me, please.	좀 도와 주세요.	chom to·wa chu·se·yo
What time is it?	지금 몇시입니까?	chi·gŭm myŏt·shi·im·ni·ka
one/first	하나/첫째	ha·na/ch'ŏt·chae
two/second	둘/둘째	tul/tul·chae
three/third	셋/세째	set/se·chae
What does this mean? I don't understand.	이것이 무슨 뜻입니까? 모르겠읍니다.	i·gŏ·shi mu·sŭn tŭ·shim·ni·ka? mo·rŭ·ge·ssŭm·ni·da
Do you speak English?	영어를 할 줄 아십니까?	yŏng·ŏ·rŭl hal chul a·shim·ni·ka

ARRIVAL

Arrival

You've arrived. Whether you've come by ship or plane, you'll have to go through passport and customs formalities.

There's bound to be somebody around who speaks English. That's why we're making this section brief. What you want is to be off to your hotel or on your way in the shortest possible time. Here are the stages for a speedy departure.

Passport control

Here's my passport.	이것이 저의 여권입니다.	i·gŏ·shi chŏ·ŭi yŏ·kwŏn·im·ni·da
I'll be staying . . .	…간 묵을 예정입니다.	. . . kan mu·gŭl ye·jŏng·im·ni·da
a few days	2, 3 일	i · sa · mil
a week	1 주일	il·chu·il
two weeks	2 주일	i·ju·il
a month	1 개월	il·gae·wŏl
I don't know yet.	아직은 모르겠읍니다.	a·ji·gŭn mo·rŭ·ge·ssŭm·ni·da
I'm here on holiday.	휴가로 왔읍니다.	hyu·ga·ro wa·ssŭm·ni·da
I'm here on business.	일 때문에 왔읍니다.	il tae·mu·ne wa·ssŭm·ni·da
I'm just passing through.	지나는 길에 들렀을 뿐 입니다.	chi·na·nŭn ki·re tŭl·lŏ·ssŭl pun·im·ni·da

If things become difficult:

I'm sorry. I don't understand. Is there anyone here who speaks English ?	미안합니다. 모르겠는데 요. 여기 영어하시는 분 계십니까 ?	mi·an·ham·ni·da. mo·rŭ·gen·nŭn·de·yo. yŏ·gi yŏng·ŏ ha·shi·nŭn pun kye·shim·ni·ka

Customs

Believe it or not, the customs officials are just as eager to wave you through as you are to go.

The chart below shows you what you can bring in duty-free.

Cigarettes	Cigars	Tobacco	Liquor (spirits)	Wine
200 and	50 or	500 grams	1l or	1l

In Korean airports, with the exception of VIPs, everyone's baggage is subject to inspection. After inspection, you should take your luggage and go through the entrance marked "Non-residents".

I have nothing to declare.	신고할 것은 아무것도 없읍니다.	shin·go·hal gŏ·sŭn a·mu·gŏt·to ŏp·sŭm·ni·da
I have ...	…을 갖고 있읍니다.	... ŭl kat·ko i·ssŭm·ni·da
400 cigarettes	궐련 400 개비	kwŏl·lyŏn sa·baek kae·bi
a bottle of whisky	위스키 한 병	wi·sŭ·ki han pyŏng
a bottle of wine	포도주 한 병	p'o·do·ju han pyŏng.
Must I pay duty on this?	세금을 내지 않으면 안됩니까?	se·gŭm·ŭl nae·ji a·nŭ·myŏn an·doem·ni·ka
How much?	얼맙니까?	ŏl·mam·ni·ka
It's for my personal use/It's not new.	그것은 제가 쓰는 것입니다. 신품이 아닙니다.	kŭ·gŏ·sŭn che·ga ssŭ·nŭn gŏ·shim·ni·da. shin·p'um·i a·nim·ni·da

Baggage — Porters

If you are lucky enough to find a porter, you can ask him to bring your luggage to customs for you. Otherwise you can usually find baggage trolleys (carts).

Porter!	포터!	p'o·t'ŏ
Can you help me with my luggage?	짐 좀 운반해 주시겠어요?	chim·jom un·ban·hae chu·shi·ge·ssŏ·yo
That's mine.	그것은 내것입니다.	kŭ·gŏ·sŭn nae·gŏ·shim·ni·da
That's my ...	그것은 나의 …입니다.	kŭ·gŏ·sŭn na·ŭi ... im·ni·da
bag/luggage/ suitcase	백/수하물/가방	paek/su·ha·mul/ka·bang
That ... one.	저 …것.	chŏ ...gŏt
big/small	큰/작은	k'ŭn/cha·gŭn
blue/brown/black	푸른/갈색의/검은	pu·rŭn/kal·sae·gŭi/kŏm·ŭn
There's one missing.	하나가 없군요.	ha·na·ga ŏp·kun·yo
Take these bags to the ...	이 백을 …로 갖다 주세요.	i bae·gŭl ... ro kat·ta chu·se·yo
taxi/bus/luggage lockers	택시/버스/수하물 보관소	t'aek·si/bŏ·sŭ/su·ha·mul po·gwan·so
Get me a taxi, please.	택시를 불러 주세요.	t'aek·si·rŭl pul·lŏ chu·se·yo
Where's the bus for the air terminal?	공항 터미널로 가는 버스는 어디서 탑니까?	kong·hang t'ŏ·mi·nŏl·lo ka·nŭn bŏ·sŭ·nŭn ŏ·di·sŏ t'am·ni·ka
How much is that?	저것은 얼마입니까?	chŏ·gŏ·sŭn ŏl·ma·im·ni·ka

ARRIVAL

Changing money

Foreign currency and traveller's cheques (checks) can be exchanged or cashed only at authorized exchange offices. Most hotel exchange counters stay open in the evening, and the airport bank is open from 6.30 a.m. to 7.30 p.m. Personal cheques are not usually accepted. For more detailed information, see pages 134–136.

Where's the nearest currency exchange?	가장 가까운 환전소는 어 딤니까?	ka·jang ka·ka·un hwan· jŏn·so·nŭn ŏ·dim·ni·ka
Can you change a traveller's cheque (check)?	여행자 수표를 바꿀 수 있읍니까?	yŏ·haeng·ja su·p'yo·rŭl pa· kul·su i·ssŭm·ni·ka
I want to change some ...	···를 환전하고 싶은데요.	... rŭl hwan·jŏn·ha·go shi· p'ŭn·de·yo
traveller's cheques	여행자 수표	yŏ·haeng·ja su·p'yo
dollars	달러	dal·lŏ
pounds	파운드	p'a·un·dŭ

Directions

How do I get to ...?	···에는 어떻게 가면 됩니까?	... e·nŭn ŏ·tŏ·ke ka·myŏn doem·ni·ka
Is there a bus into town?	시내로 가는 버스가 있읍니까?	shi·nae·ro ka·nŭn bŏ·sŭ·ga i·ssŭm·ni·ka
Where can I get a taxi?	택시는 어디서 탑니까?	t'aek·si·nŭn ŏ·di·sŏ t'am· ni·ka
Where can I rent a car?	자동차는 어디서 빌릴 수 있읍니까?	cha·dong·ch'a·nŭn ŏ·di·sŏ pil·lil·su i·ssŭm·ni·ka

Hotel reservations

Obviously, it is safest to book in advance if you can. But if you haven't done so?
Personnel of the Korean Tourist Corporation and the Korean Tourist Association can be found in the main hall of airports — look for the sign marked ''Hotel Information Centre''. You will be able to make hotel reservations there anytime between 6 a.m. and 10 p.m.

FOR NUMBERS, see page 175

Car rental

Again, it's best to make arrangements in advance whenever possible. There are car rental firms in major cities. You are almost certain to find someone there who speaks English. But if not, try one of the following . . .

I'd like . . .	…를 빌리고 싶은데요.	. . . rŭl pil·li·go shi·p'ŭn·de·yo
a car	자동차	cha·dong·ch'a
a small car	소형 자동차	so·hyŏng cha·dong·ch'a
a large car	대형 자동차	tae·hyŏng cha·dong·ch'a
a sports car	스포츠카	sŭ·p'o·ch'ŭ·k'a
I would like it for . . .	…을 빌리고 싶은데요.	. . . ŭl pil·li·go shi·p'ŭn·de·yo
a day/four days	하루/4 일	ha·ru/sa·il
a week/two weeks	1 주일/2 주일	il·chu·il/i·ju·il
What's the charge per day ?	하루에 요금이 얼마입니까 ?	ha·ru·e yo·gŭ·mi ŏl·ma·im·ni·ka
What's the charge per week ?	1 주일에 요금이 얼마입니까 ?	il·chu·i·re yo·gŭ·mi ŏl·ma·im·ni·ka
Does that include mileage ?	마일수도 포함되어 있읍니까 ?	ma·il·su·do p'o·ham·doe·ŏ i·ssŭm·ni·ka
Is petrol (gasoline) included ?	휘발유값도 포함되어 있읍니까 ?	hwi·bal·yu·gap·to p'o·ham·doe·ŏ i·ssŭm·ni·ka
Does that include full insurance ?	보험료도 모두 포함되어 있읍니까 ?	po·hŏm·ryo·do mo·du p'o·ham·doe·ŏ i·ssŭm·ni·ka
What's the deposit ?	보증금은 얼마입니까 ?	po·jŭng·gŭ·mŭn ŏl·ma·im·ni·ka
I have a credit card.	크레디트 카드를 갖고 있는데요.	k'ŭ·re·di·t'ŭ k'a·dŭ·rŭl kat·ko in·nŭn·de·yo
Here's my driving licence.	이것이 나의 운전 면허증입니다.	i·gŏ·shi na·ŭi un·jŏn myŏn·hŏ·jŭng·im·ni·da

Note : If you have an International Driving Licence, you may drive in Korea at any time. If, however, your licence is restricted to your country of origin, you will have to apply for a Korean driving permit before being allowed to drive in Korea.

FOR SIGHTSEEING, see page 75

Taxi

All taxis have meters. It is usually best to ask the approximate fare beforehand. From 12 p.m. to 4 a.m. there is a supplementary fare, which is indicated on the meter. No tip is required. In large cities you will find two types of taxi: Mid-size and Deluxe. Mid-size taxis have a blue light on the roof and Deluxe have a yellow light. The fare for a Deluxe taxi is about twice that of standard taxis.

Where can I get a taxi?	택시는 어디서 탈 수 있습니까?	t'aek·si·nŭn ŏ·di·sŏ t'al·su i·ssŭm·ni·ka
Get me a taxi, please.	택시를 불러 주세요.	t'aek·si·rŭl pul·lŏ chu·se·yo
What's the fare to ...?	…까지 요금이 얼마입니까?	... ka·ji yo·gŭ·mi ŏl·ma·im·ni·ka
How far is it to ...?	…까지 얼마나 멉니까?	... ka·ji ŏl·ma·na mŏm·ni·ka
Take me to ...?	…까지 태워다 주세요.	... ka·ji t'ae·wŏ·da chu·se·yo
this address	이 주소	i chu·so
the centre of town	도심지	to·shim·ji
the ... Hotel	…호텔	... ho·t'el
Go straight ahead.	똑바로 가주세요.	tok·pa·ro ka·ju·se·yo
Turn ... at the next corner.	다음 모퉁이에서 …으로 돌아 주세요.	ta·ŭm mo·t'ung·i·e·sŏ ... ŭ·ro to·ra chu·se·yo
left/right	왼쪽/오른쪽	oen·chok/o·rŭn·chok
Stop here, please.	여기서 세워 주세요.	yŏ·gi·sŏ se·wŏ chu·se·yo
I'm in a hurry.	시간이 급합니다.	shi·ga·ni kŭp·ham·ni·da
There's no hurry.	급하게 가지 않아도 됩니다.	kŭp·ha·ge ka·ji a·na·do doem·ni·da
Could you drive more slowly?	좀 더 천천히 운전해 주시겠어요?	chom·dŏ ch'ŏn·ch'ŏn·hi un·jŏn·hae chu·shi·ge·ssŏ·yo

Hotel—Inn—Other accommodation

Early reservation (and confirmation) is essential in most major tourist centres during the high season. Most towns and arrival points have a Korean Tourist Association (*han·guk kwan·gwang hyŏp·hoe*) office, and that's the place to go to if you're stuck without a room.

In Korea, you can choose between two totally different types of hotels: Western-style and Korean-style. The latter is generally cheaper.

Western-style hotels

In major Korean cities and tourist resorts there are many Western-style hotels which maintain quality standards comparable to modern hotels in Europe or the U.S. They range from luxury class down to modest hotels.

Korean-style inns (yŏ·gwan)

Staying at a *yŏ·gwan*, besides being cheaper than staying in a Western-style hotel, will enable you to sample a bit of Korean life: Korean atmosphere, Korean bath, Korean bed, etc. The *yŏ·gwans* look practically the same as ordinary Korean houses except that they are much larger. You will also receive personal service and attention akin to the hospitality of a Korean family. Prices are for room only.

There are currently over 30,000 *yŏ·gwans* in Korea, of which about 3,000 have facilities for handling Western visitors, such as individual bathrooms and Western-style washrooms. They can also prepare simple Western-style meals. The overwhelming majority of the *yŏ·gwans,* however, are not accustomed to catering to Western guests, but, precisely for this reason, staying n one of the smaller *yŏgwans* may be an exciting way to spend your time in Korea in the real Korean way.

f you would like to see how the Koreans really live, you can arrange to stay with a Korean family as a paying guest by contacting Tourist Information Centres in major Korean cities. In this section, we are mainly concerned with the smaller and middle-class hotels and inns. You'll have no language difficulties in the luxury and first-class hotels where at least some of the staff have been trained to speak English.

In the next few pages we shall consider your requirements—step by step—from arrival to departure. There's no need to read through the whole lot. Just turn to the situation that applies.

Checking in—Reception

My name is . . .	내 이름은 …입니다.	nae i·rŭm·ŭn . . . im·ni·da
I have a reservation.	예약을 했읍니다.	ye·ya·gŭl hae·ssŭm·ni·da
We have reserved two rooms, a single and a double.	1인용 방 하나와 2인용 방 하나를 예약했읍니다.	i·rin·yong pang ha·na·wa i·in·yong pang ha·na·rŭl ye·yak·hae·ssŭm·ni·da
I wrote to you last month. Here's the confirmation.	지난달에 편지로 예약했어요. 이것이 그 확인증입니다.	chi·nan·da·re p'yŏn·ji·ro ye·yak·hae·ssŏ·yo. i·gŏ·shi kŭ hwa·gin·jŭng·im·ni·da
I'd like . . .	…을 주세요.	. . . ŭl chu·se·yo
a single room	1인용 방	i·rin·yong pang
a double room	2인용 방	i·in·yong pang
two single rooms	1인용 방 둘	i·rin·yong pang dul
a room with twin beds	침대 둘 있는 방	ch'im·dae dul in·nŭn pang
a room with a bath	욕실이 달린 방	yok·shi·ri tal·lin pang
a room with a shower	샤워가 달린 방	sha·wŏ·ga tal·lin pang
a room with a balcony	발코니가 있는 방	bal·k'o·ni·ga in·nŭn pang
a room with a view	경치가 좋은 방	kyŏng·ch'i·ga cho·ŭn pang
a suite	두개가 붙은 방	tu·gae·ga pu·t'ŭn pang

We'd like a room ...	…방을 원합니다.	... pang·ŭl wŏn·ham· ni·da·man
in the front/at the back	앞쪽의/뒤쪽의	ap·cho·gǔi/twi·cho·gǔi
facing the sea	바다를 향한	pa·da·rǔl hyang·han
facing the courtyard	안마당을 향한	an·ma·dang·ŭl hyang·han
It must be quiet.	조용한 방을 부탁합니다.	cho·yong·han pang·ŭl pu· t'ak·ham·ni·da
I'd rather have something higher up (lower down).	위층(아래층)을 희망합니 다.	wi·ch'ǔng·(a·rae·ch'ǔng)·ǔl hǔi·mang·ham·ni·da
Is there ...?	…이 있나요?	... i in·na·yo
air conditioning/ heating	냉방 장치/난방 장치	naeng·bang chang·ch'i/ nan·bang chang·ch'i
hot water/running water	온수/수도	on·su/su·do
a laundry/valet service	세탁소/급사의 시중	se·t'ak·so/kǔp·sa·ǔi shi· jung
a private toilet	개인용 화장실	kae·in·yong hwa·jang·shil
a radio/television in the room	방에 라디오/텔레비전	pang·e ra·di·o/t'el·le·bi·jŏn

How much?

What's the price ...?	…의 요금은 얼마입니 까?	... ŭi yo·gǔ·mǔn ŏl·ma· im·ni·ka
per night/per week	하룻밤/1주일	ha·rut·pam/il·chu·il
for bed and breakfast	아침 식사를 포함한 숙박	a·ch'im shik·sa·rǔl p'o·ham·han suk·pak
excluding meals	식사 제외	shik·sa che·oe
for full board	세끼 포함	se·ki p'o·ham
Does that include ...?	…가 포함되어 있읍니 까?	... ga p'o·ham·doe·ŏ i· ssǔm·ni·ka
breakfast/meals/ service	아침 식사/식사/서비스	a·ch'im shik·sa/shik·sa/ sŏ·bi·sǔ
Is there any reduction for children?	어린이의 할인이 있읍니 까?	ŏ·ri·ni·ǔi ha·ri·ni i·ssǔm·ni·ka

Do you charge for the baby?	어린애도 계산에 넣습니까?	ŏ·ri·nae·do kye·sa·ne nŏt·sŭm·ni·ka
That's too expensive.	너무 비쌉니다.	nŏ·mu pi·ssam·ni·da
Haven't you anything cheaper?	더 싼 방은 없읍니까?	tŏ ssan pang·ŭn ŏp·sŭm·ni·ka

How long?

We'll be staying . . .	…숙박하겠읍니다.	. . . suk·pak·ha·ge·ssŭm·ni·da
overnight only/a few days	하룻밤만/2, 3 일	ha·rut·pam·man/i·sa·mil
a week (at least)	(적어도) 1주일	(chŏ·gŏ·do) il·chu·il
I don't know yet.	아직 모르겠읍니다.	a·jik mo·rŭ·ge·ssŭm·ni·da

Decision

May I see the room?	방을 보여 주시겠읍니까?	pang·ŭl po·yŏ chu·shi·ge·ssŭm·ni·ka
No, I don't like it.	마음에 안듭니다.	ma·ŭ·me an·dŭm·ni·da
It's too . . .	너무 …(합니다).	nŏ·mu . . . (ham·ni·da)
cold/hot	춥습니다/덥습니다	ch'up·sŭm·ni·da/tŏp·sŭm·ni·da
dark/small/noisy	어둡습니다/작습니다/시끄럽습니다	ŏ·dup·sŭm·ni·da/chak·sŭm·ni·da/shi·kŭ·rŏp·sŭm·ni·da
No, that won't do at all.	저래 가지고는 안되겠읍니다.	chŏ·rae ka·ji·go·nŭn an·doe·ge·ssŭm·ni·da
Have you anything . . . ?	…한 것은 없읍니까?	. . . han kŏ·sŭn ŏp·sŭm·ni·ka
better/bigger	더 좋은/더 큰	tŏ cho·ŭn/tŏ k'ŭn
cheaper/smaller	더 싼/더 작은	tŏ ssan/tŏ cha·gŭn
Have you a room with a better view?	경치가 더 좋은 방이 있읍니까?	kyŏng·ch'i·ga tŏ cho·ŭn pang·i i·ssŭm·ni·ka
That's fine. I'll take it.	좋습니다. 이걸로 하지요.	cho·ssŭm·ni·da i·gŏl·lo ha·ji·yo

FOR NUMBERS, see page 176

HOTEL

Bills

These are usually paid weekly, or on departure if you stay less than a week. In general, there is no room charge for children under six accompanying adults.

Tipping

A service charge varying between 10% and 15% is normally included in the bill. But you can ask: *sŏ·bi·sŭ·ryo·nŭn tŭ·rŏ i·ssŭm·ni·ka ?* (Is service included ?) Tip the porter when he brings the bags to your room. Also tip the bellboy if he does any errands for you. Otherwise, however, tipping is not customary in Korea.

Registration

Upon arrival at a hotel you will be asked to fill in a registration form. It asks your name, home address, passport number and further destination. It's almost certain to carry an English translation. However, if you stay in a Korean-style hotel (*yŏ·gwan*), especially in the country, they may have it only in Korean. Then you ask:

What does this mean ?	이것은 무슨 뜻입니까 ?	i·gŏ·sŭn mu·sŭn tŭ·shim·ni·ka

You will probably be asked for your passport. It may be kept for a while, even overnight. Don't worry—you'll get it back. And some of these questions could come up:

여권을 보여 주시겠읍니까 ?	May I see your passport ?
이 숙박부에 기입해 주시겠읍니까 ?	Would you mind filling in this registration form ?
여기에 서명해 주세요.	Sign here, please.
얼마나 숙박하시겠읍니까 ?	How long will you be staying ?

FOR TIPPING, see page 1

HOTEL

Service, please

Now that you are safely installed, meet some more of the hotel staff:

the bellboy	급사	kŭp·sa
the maid	객실 하녀	kaek·shil ha·nyŏ
the manager	지배인	chi·bae·in
the telephone operator	전화 교환수	chŏn·hwa kyo·hwan·su

General requirements

Please ask the maid to come up.	객실하녀에게 오라고 해 주세요.	kaek·shil ha·nyŏ·e·ge o·ra·go hae·ju·se·yo
Who is it?	누구십니까?	nu·gu·shim·ni·ka
Just a minute.	잠깐 기다려 주세요.	cham·kan ki·da·ryŏ chu·se·yo
Come in.	들어 오세요.	tŭ·rŏ o·se·yo
The door's open.	문은 열려 있습니다.	mu·nŭn yŏl·lyŏ i·ssŭm·ni·da
Is there a bath on this floor?	이 층에 목욕탕이 있습니까?	i ch'ŭng·e mo·gyok·t'ang·i i·ssŭm·ni·ka

Note : If you stay in a *yŏgwan* (Korean-style inn) in the country, there may be only one large bathroom available which you'll have to share with other guests.

How does this shower work?	이 샤워는 어떻게 사용합니까?	i sha·wŏ·nŭn ŏ·tŏ·ke sa·yong·ham·ni·ka
Where's the socket (outlet) for a shaver?	전기 면도기용의 콘센트는 어디에 있습니까?	chŏn·gi myŏn·do·gi·yong·ŭi k'on·sen·t'ŭ·nŭn ŏ·di·e i·ssŭm·ni·ka
What's the voltage?	전압은 몇 볼트입니까?	chŏ·na·bŭn myŏt pol·t'ŭ·im·ni·ka

HOTEL-SERVICE

Please send up ...	···을 보내 주세요.	... ŭl po·nae chu·se·yo
two coffees/ sandwiches/ gin and tonics	커피 2잔/샌드위치 2개/ 진토닉 2잔	k'ŏ·p'i tu·jan/saen·dŭ·wi· ch'i tu·gae/chin·t'o·nik tu·jan
Can we have break- fast in our room ?	방에서 아침 식사를 할 수 있읍니까?	pang·e·sŏ a·ch'im shik·sa· rŭl hal·su i·ssŭm·ni·ka
I'd like to leave these in your safe.	이것들을 금고에 맡기고 싶은데요.	i·gŏt·dŭl·ŭl kŭm·go·e mat· ki·go ship·p'ŭn·de·yo
Can you find me a baby-sitter ?	아이 보는 사람을 구해줄 수 있어요?	a·i po·nŭn sa·ra·mŭl ku·hae· jul·su i·ssŏ·yo
May I have a/an/ some ... ?	···을 주시겠어요?	... ŭl chu·shi·ge·ssŏ·yo
ashtray	재떨이	chae·tŏ·ri
bath towel	목욕 수건	mo·gyok su·gŏn
extra blanket	담요를 한 장 더	tam·nyo·rŭl han·jang tŏ
envelopes	봉투	pong·t'u
(more) hangers	옷걸이(를 더)	ot·kŏ·ri (rŭl tŏ)
comb	빗	pit
ice	얼음	ŏ·rŭm
needle and thread	바늘과 실	pa·nŭl·gwa shil
extra pillow	베개를 하나 더	pe·gae·rŭl ha·na tŏ
reading-lamp	전기 스탠드	chŏn·gi sŭ·t'aen·dŭ
soap	비누	pi·nu
writing-paper	편지지	p'yŏn·ji·ji
Where's the ... ?	···은 어딥니까?	... ŭn ŏ·dim·ni·ka
bathroom	욕실	yok·shil
beauty parlour	미장원	mi·jang·wŏn
cocktail lounge	주점	chu·jŏm
dining room	식당	shik·tang
hairdresser's	이발소	i·bal·so
perfume shop	화장품점	hwa·jang·p'um·jŏm
restaurant	음식점	ŭm·shik·chŏm
television room	텔레비전이 있는 방	t'el·le·bi·jŏn·i in·nŭn pang
toilet	화장실	hwa·jang·shil

Breakfast

If you stay in a Korean-style hotel (*yŏ.gwan*), you will be offered the standard Korean breakfast consisting of a bowl of rice, soy bean soup, seaweed, cooked greens, etc. If this does not appeal to you, you may order a Western-style breakfast the night before. In cheaper *yŏ.gwans* or in *yŏ.gwans* in the country, however, it is advisable not to do so, as they may not know how to prepare a Western-style breakfast. At Western-style hotels you'll have no problem. They provide Continental, English or American breakfasts.

I'll have a/an/ some ...	···을 주세요.	... ŭl chu·se·yo
bacon and eggs	베이컨과 계란	be·i·k'ŏn·gwa kye·ran
cereal	시리얼	si·ri·ŏl
hot/cold	뜨거운/찬	tŭ·gŏ·un/ch'an
eggs	계란	kye·ran
boiled egg	삶은 계란	sal·mŭn kye·ran
soft/medium/hard	설 익힌/반숙한/ 푹 삶은	sŏl i·k'in/pan·suk·han/ p'uk sal·mŭn
fried	프라이한	p'ŭ·ra·i·han
scrambled	풀어서 볶은	p'u·rŏ·sŏ po·kŭn
fruit juice	프루트 쥬스	p'ŭ·ru·t'ŭ chyu·sŭ
grapefruit/orange	그레이프프루트/오렌지	gŭ·re·i·p'ŭ·p'ŭ·ru·t'ŭ/ o·ren·ji
pineapple/tomato	파인애플/도마도	p'a·in·ae·p'ŭl/to·ma·do
ham and eggs	햄 에그	haem e·gŭ
omelet	오믈렛	o·mŭl·let
sausages	소세지	so·se·ji
May I have some ...?	···을 주시겠어요?	... ŭl chu·shi·ge·ssŏ·yo
hot/cold milk	뜨거운/찬 우유	tŭ·gŏ·un/ch'an u·yu
cream/sugar	크림/설탕	k'ŭ·rim/sŏl·t'ang
more butter	버터를 좀 더	bŏ·t'ŏ·rŭl chom tŏ
salt/pepper	소금/후추	so·gŭm/hu·ch'u
coffee/tea	커피/홍차	k'ŏ·p'i/ĥong·ch'a
chocolate	초콜렛	ch'o·k'ol·let
lemon/honey	레몬/꿀	le·mon/kul

HOTEL-SERVICE

Could you bring me a...?	…을 갖다 주시겠어요?	…ŭl kat·ta chu·shi·ge·ssŏ·yo
cup	컵	k'ŏp
fork	포크	p'o·k'ŭ
knife	나이프	na·i·p'ŭ
plate	접시	chŏp·shi
spoon	스푼	sŭ·p'un

Note : You'll find a great many other dishes listed in our guide "Eating out" (pages 39-64). This should be consulted for your lunch and dinner menus.

Difficulties

The ... doesn't work.	…이 고장났어요.	…i ko·jang·na·ssŏ·yo
air-conditioner	에어콘	e·ŏ·k'on
fan	선풍기	sŏn·p'ung·gi
faucet	수도 꼭지	su·do kok·chi
heating	난방 장치	nan·bang chang·ch'i
light	전등	chŏn·dŭng
tap	수도 꼭지	su·do kok·chi
toilet	화장실	hwa·jang·shil
ventilator	환풍기	hwan·p'ung·gi
The wash-basin is clogged.	세면대가 막혔어요.	se·myŏn·dae·ga ma·k'yŏ·ssŏ·yo
The window is jammed.	창문이 움직이지 않아요.	ch'ang·mu·ni um·ji·gi·ji a·na·yo
The blind is stuck.	블라인드가 움직이지 않아요.	bŭl·la·in·dŭ·ga um·ji·gi·ji a·na·yo
These aren't my shoes.	이것은 내 구두가 아닙니다.	i·gŏ·sŭn nae ku·du·ga a·nim·ni·da
This isn't my laundry.	이것은 내 세탁물이 아닙니다.	i·gŏ·sŭn nae se·t'ak·mu·ri a·nim·ni·da
There's no hot water.	뜨거운 물이 안나와요.	tŭ·gŏ·un mu·ri an·na·wa·yo
I've lost my ...	…을 잃어버렸어요.	…ŭl i·rŏ·bŏ·ryŏ·ssŏ·yo
watch/key	시계/열쇠	shi·gye/yŏl·soe

I've left my key in my room.	열쇠를 방에 놓고 문을 잠갔어요.	yŏl·soe·rŭl pang·e no·k'o mu·nŭl cham·ga·ssŏ·yo
The ... is broken.	…이 깨졌어요.	... i kae·jyŏ·ssŏ·yo
bulb	전구	chŏn·gu
lamp	전등	chŏn·dŭng
plug	플러그	p'ŭl·lŏ·gŭ
shutter	셔터	shyŏ·t'ŏ
switch	스위치	sŭ·wi·ch'i
venetian blind	블라인드	bŭl·la·in·dŭ
window shade	차양	ch'a·yang
Can you get it fixed?	그것을 고쳐줄수 있읍니까?	kŭ·gŏ·sŭl ko·ch'yŏ·jul·su i·ssŭm·ni·ka
Can you replace it?	그것을 바꿔줄수 있읍니까?	kŭ·gŏ·sŭl pa·kwŏ·jul·su i·ssŭm·ni·ka

Telephone—Mail—Callers

Can you get me Seoul 123 4567?	서울 123 국 4567 번을 부탁합니다.	sŏ·ul il·i·sam·guk sa·o·yuk·ch'il·bŏ·nŭl pu·t'ak·ham·ni·da
Did anyone call me?	나한테 전화 온 데 있읍니까?	na·han·t'e chŏn·hwa on de i·ssŭm·ni·ka
Operator, I've been cut off.	교환양, 전화가 끊어졌어요.	kyo·hwan·yang, chŏn·hwa·ga kŭ·nŏ·jŏ·ssŏ·yo
Is there any mail for me?	나한테 우편물 온 것 있읍니까?	na·han·t'e u·p'yŏn·mul on kŏt i·ssŭm·ni·ka
Have you any stamps?	우표 있읍니까?	u·p'yo i·ssŭm·ni·ka
Would you mail this for me, please?	이것을 우편으로 부쳐 주시겠어요?	i·gŏ·sŭl u·p'yŏn·ŭ·ro pu·ch'ŏ chu·shi·ge·ssŏ·yo
Are there any messages for me?	나한테 무슨 전갈이 없읍니까?	na·han·t'e mu·sŭn chŏn·ga·ri ŏp·ssŭm·ni·ka

FOR POST OFFICE, see page 137

Checking out

May I have my bill, please ? Room 398.	계산서를 주시겠어요? 398 호실입니다.	kye·san·sŏ·rŭl chu·shi·ge·ssŏ·yo? 398 ho·shil·im·ni·da
I'm leaving early tomorrow. Please have my bill ready.	내일 일찍 떠납니다. 계산서를 준비해 주세요.	nae·il il·chik tŏ·nam·ni·da kye·san·sŏ·rŭl chun·bi·hae chu·se·yo
We'll be checking out ...	…체크 아웃합니다.	... ch'e·k'ŭ a·ut·ham·ni·da
around noon/soon	점심때쯤/곧	chŏm·shim·tae·chŭm/kot
I must leave at once.	지금 곧 떠나지 않으면 안돼요.	chi·gŭm kot tŏ·na·ji a·nŭ·myŏn an·dwe·yo
Does this include...?	…은 들어 있습니까?	... ŭn tŭ·rŏ i·ssŭm·ni·ka
service/tax	서비스료/세금	sŏ·bi·sŭ·ryo/se·gŭm
Is everything included ?	전부 들어 있습니까?	chŏn·bu tŭ·rŏ i·ssŭm·ni·ka
You've made a mistake in this bill, I think.	계산서가 틀린 것 같은데 요.	kye·san·sŏ·ga t'ul·lin kŏt ka·t'ŭn·de·yo
It's too high. It's ridiculous.	너무 비싸군요. 터무니없 어요.	nŏ·mu pi·ssa·gun·yo t'ŏ·mu·ni ŏp·sŏ·yo
Can you get me a taxi?	택시를 잡아 주시겠어 요?	t'aek·shi·rŭl cha·ba chu·shi·ge·ssŏ·yo
Would you send someone to bring down our baggage ?	짐을 갖고 내려가야겠는 데 누구 좀 보내주겠어 요?	chim·ŭl kat·ko nae·ryŏ·ga·ya·gen·nŭn·de nu·gu chom po·nae·ju·ge·ssŏ·yo
We're in a great hurry.	우린 매우 급합니다.	u·rin mae·u kŭp·ham·ni·da
Here's the forwarding address. You have my home address.	이것이 다음에 갈 주소입 니다. 우리집 주소는 알 고 계시지요?	i·gŏ·shi ta·ŭ·me kal chu·so·im·ni·da. u·ri·jip chu·so·nŭn al·go gye·shi·ji·yo
It's been a very enjoyable stay.	매우 즐겁게 지냈습니다.	mae·u chŭl·gŏp·ke chi·nae·ssŭm·ni·da
I hope we'll come again sometime.	다음에 또 오겠읍니다.	ta·ŭm·e to o·ge·ssŭm·ni·da

FOR TAXI, see page 27

Eating out

There are many types of eating and drinking places in Korea. Going to a restaurant in Korea is very much like going to a restaurant in the West, but there are some that specialize in dishes like *pul·go·gi, chŏn·gol, kal·bi* or *hoe*; so, pay attention to what kind of restaurant you're entering. If you wish, you can reserve a private dining room in a Korean-style restaurant. Having taken your shoes off at the entrance, you will be seated on soft cushions placed on the *ondol* (heated floor). Or you may prefer to sit at a Western-style table which can now be found in most Korean restaurants.

비어 홀 *(pi·ŏ hol)*	Beer hall. Beer and snacks served. Some halls also offer live entertainment.
바 *(pa)*	Bar. Drinks and snacks served. Most bars have many hostesses, and you'll have to pay for their drinks, too.
다방 *(ta·bang)*	Coffee shop. Coffee, soft drinks and snacks are served. All coffee shops have music, and are very popular throughout Korea.
레스토랑 *(re·sŭ·t'o·rang)*	Most restaurants serve both Korean and Ko-reanized Western-style food. Alternatively, in major cities like Seoul and Pusan you'll find restaurants of many different nationalities.

한식집
(han·shik·jip)

Specializes in Korean-style food only. Try one of these: *pul·go·gi, chŏn·gol, kal·bi, pi·bim·bap.* Korean-style restaurants may generally be divided into two kinds: those which are large in size and offer luxurious cuisine along with entertainment, and those which just serve food at ordinary prices. The luxury-type restaurants usually have the suffix "*Kwan*" affixed to the restaurant's own particular name, and offer private rooms with hostess service. Usually, wine or beer is served with the food. For entertainment at this type of restaurant, prior reservations are recommended. Though private rooms are also available at regular-type restaurants, dining hall service with tables and chairs is more usual.

스낵집
(sŭ·naek·jip)

Reasonably-priced fast-food restaurants are generally found around universities and other places where young people tend to congregate in large numbers.

Many restaurants display wax representations of their dishes together with the prices in glass cases facing the street.

Meal times

Breakfast (*a·ch'im*) : until 9 a.m.

Lunch (*chŏm·shim*) : from noon to 2 p.m.

Dinner (*chŏ·nyŏk*) : from 6 p.m. to 9 p.m.

To get a table in a well-known restaurant, telephone in advance:

I'd like to reserve a table for four, for 8 o'clock tonight.	오늘밤 8시에 4인용 테이블을 예약하고자 하는데요.	o·nŭl·bam yŏ·dŏl·shi·e sa·in·yong t'e·i·bŭl·ŭl ye·yak·ha·go·ja ha·nŭn·de·yo

A few words on Korean table manners

The Koreans eat with spoons and chopsticks. How to use chopsticks can be briefly explained as follows: you hold the upper stick between your thumb and first two fingers, while you keep the lower stick stationary with your third finger or both your second and third fingers; and you hold the sticks one third above the hand and two thirds below.

Korean restaurants will usually bring you a pair of wooden half-split chopsticks in paper envelopes. You can easily split them into two. In Korean homes, however, permanently re-usable sticks are used. Such chopsticks are nowadays often made of plastic.

Korean table manners have changed considerably since the 1970s. Now, as Korea has become more westernized, making noises while eating would be considered bad-mannered and even offensive to other people at the table.

In Korean homes and restaurants you will find both chairs and tables as well as the traditional *ondol* (heated floor) with silk-covered cushions.

Hungry?

I'm hungry/I'm thirsty.	배가 고픕니다/목이 마릅니다.	pae·ga ko·p'ŭm·ni·da/mo·gi ma·rŭm·ni·da
Can you recommend a good (and inexpensive) restaurant?	좋은(그리고 비싸지 않은) 음식점을 소개해 주시겠어요?	cho·hŭn (kŭ·ri·go pi·ssa·ji a·nŭn) ŭm·shik·chŏm·ŭl so·gae·hae chu·shi·ge·ssŏ·yo

Asking and ordering

Good evening. I'd like a table for 3.	안녕하십니까. 3인용 테이블이 있읍니까?	an·nyŏng·ha·shim·ni·ka. 3·in·yong t'e·i·bŭl·i i·ssŭm·ni·ka
Could we have a . . . ?	···이 있읍니까?	. . . i i·ssŭm·ni·ka
table in the corner	구석의 테이블	ku·sŏ·gŭi t'e·i·bŭl
table by the window	창가의 테이블	ch'ang·ka·ŭi t'e·i·bŭl
table outside	바깥쪽 테이블	pa·kat·chok t'e·i·bŭl
table on the terrace	테라스의 테이블	t'e·ra·sŭ·ŭi t'e·i·bŭl
Where are the toilets?	화장실이 어딥니까?	hwa·jang·shi·ri ŏ·dim·ni·ka
Can you serve me right away? I'm in a hurry.	금방 주실 수 있어요? 지금 급합니다.	kŭm·bang chu·shil·su i·ssŏ·yo? chi·gŭm kŭp·ham·ni·da
What's the price of the fixed menu?	정식은 얼마입니까?	chŏng·shi·gŭn ŏl·ma·im·ni·ka
Is service included?	서비스료도 들어 있읍니까?	sŏ·bi·sŭ·ryo·do tŭ·rŏ i·ssŭm·ni·ka
Could we have a/ an . . . , please?	···을 주시겠어요?	. . . ŭl chu·shi·ge·ssŏ·yo
ashtray	재떨이	chae·tŏ·ri
bottle of . . .	···한 병	. . . han pyŏng
another chair	다른 의자	ta·rŭn ŭi·ja
chopsticks	젓가락	chŏt·ka·rak
fork	포크	p'o·k'ŭ
glass of water	물 한 컵	mul han k'ŏp
knife	나이프	na·i·p'ŭ
napkin	냅킨	naep·k'in
plate	접시	chŏp·shi
spoon	스푼	sŭ·p'un
toothpick	이쑤시개	i·ssu·shi·gae

FOR COMPLAINTS, see page 59

I'd like a/an/some . . .	…을 주세요.	. . . ŭl chu·se·yo
aperitif	반주	pan·ju
appetizer	전채	chŏn·ch'ae
beer	맥주	maek·chu
bread	빵	pang
butter	버터	bŏ·t'ŏ
cabbage	양배추	yang·bae·ch'u
cheese	치즈	ch'i·jŭ
chips (french fries)	얇게 썬 감자 튀김	yal·ke ssŏn kam·ja t'wi·gim
coffee	커피	k'ŏ·p'i
dessert	디저트	di·jŏ·t'ŭ
fish	생선	saeng·sŏn
fruit	과일	kwa·il
game	엽조	yŏp·cho
ice-cream	아이스크림	a·i·sŭ·k'ŭ·rim
ketchup	케첩	k'e·ch'ŏp
lemon	레몬	le·mon
lettuce	상치	sang·ch'i
meat	고기	ko·gi
milk	우유	u·yu
mineral water	미네랄 워터	mi·ne·ral wŏ·t'ŏ
mustard	겨자	kyŏ·ja
oil	기름	ki·rŭm
pepper	후추	hu·ch'u
potatoes	감자	kam·ja
rice	밥	pap
rolls	로울빵	ro·ul·pang
salad	샐러드	sael·lŏ·dŭ
salt	소금	so·gŭm
sandwich	샌드위치	saen·dŭ·wi·ch'i
seasoning	조미료	cho·mi·ryo
shellfish	새우류	sae·u·ryu
snack	스낵	sŭ·naek
soup	수프	su·p'ŭ
spaghetti	스파게티	sŭ·p'a·ge·t'i
starter	전채	chŏn·ch'ae
sugar	설탕	sŏl·t'ang
tea	홍차	hong·ch'a
vegetables	채소	ch'ae·so
vinegar	식초	shik·ch'o
water	물	mul
wine	포도주	p'o·do·ju

EATING OUT

What's on the menu?

Our menu reader is presented according to courses. Under each heading you'll find an alphabetical list of dishes in Korean with their English equivalents. This serves two purposes. Firstly, it's designed to help you make the most of both Korean and Western-style menus. It includes everyday items and special dishes. Secondly, you can use the lists for personal shopping.

Here's our guide to good eating and drinking. Turn to the course you want.

Obviously, you're not going to go through every course on the menu. If you've had enough, say:

Nothing more, thanks.	다 먹었읍니다, 감사합니다.	ta mŏ·gŏ·ssŭm·ni·da kam·sa·ham·ni·da

When ordering your meal, the best way to use our guide is to show the waiter the food list (pp. 45 to 58). Let him point to what's currently available.

FOR BREAKFAST, see page 35

Appetizers—Starters

I'd like an appetizer.	전채를 주세요.	chŏn·ch'ae·rŭl chu·se·yo
What do you recommend?	뭐가 좋을까요?	mwŏ·ga cho·ŭl·ka·yo

게	ke	crabmeat
고등어	ko·dŭng·ŏ	mackerel
굴	kul	oysters
달팽이	tal·p'aeng·i	snails
대하	tae·ha	lobster
대합	tae·hap	clams
모듬전채	mo·dŭm chŏn·ch'ae	assorted appetizers
무우	mu·u	radishes
버섯	pŏ·sŏt	mushrooms
살라미	sal·la·mi	salami
샐러드	sael·lŏ·dŭ	salad
셀러리	sel·lŏ·ri	celery
소시지	so·shi·ji	sausage
수박	su·bak	watermelon
아스파라가스	a·sŭ·p'a·ra·gas	asparagus tips
앤초우비	aen·ch'o·u·bi	anchovies
어란	ŏ·ran	roe
연어	yŏn·ŏ	salmon
올리브	ol·li·bŭ	olives
작은 새우	cha·gŭn sae·u	shrimp
정어리	chŏng·ŏ·ri	sardines
중(中)새우	chung·sae·u	prawns
참치	ch'am·ch'i	tunny fish(tuna)
청어	ch'ŏng·ŏ	herring
캐비아	k'ae·bi·a	caviar
프루트 쥬스	p'ŭ·ru·tŭ chyu·sŭ	fruit juice
피만고추	p'i·man ko·ch'u	sweet (green) peppers
햄	haem	ham

Korean specialities

마른 안주
(ma·rŭn an·ju)

This is a collective name for a Korean-style appetizer. This may include many dishes, generally eaten with drinks. Ask the waiter to recommend one to you.

Salad

Salad isn't part of authentic Korean cuisine. Pickled vegetables are a more typical equivalent. However, you can order salads in Western-style restaurants.

What kinds of salad have you got?	무슨 샐러드가 있읍니까?	mu·sŭn sael·lŏ·dŭ·ga i·ssŭm·ni·ka

Soup

In the Korean meal, soup is eaten simultaneously with (never prior to) the main course (boiled rice and other items). In Western-style restaurants, however, you can have Western-style soups.

| I'd like some soup. | 수프를 주세요. | su·p'ŭ·rŭl chu·se·yo. |
| What do you recommend? | 뭐가 좋습니까? | mwŏ·ga cho·ssŭm·ni·ka |

Egg dishes and omelets

There are no specific egg dishes or omelets in authentic Korean cuisine, although eggs are very frequently used as ingredients. Omelets are an import from the West. You can have them in Western-style restaurants.

| I'd like an omelet. | 오믈렛을 주세요. | o·mŭl·ret·ŭl chu·se·yo |

Fish and seafood

I'd like some fish.	생선을 주세요.	saeng·sŏn·ŭl chu·se·yo
What kinds of shell-fish have you got?	어떤 새우류가 있읍니까 ?	ŏ·tŏn sae·u·ryu·ga i·ssŭm·ni·ka

전갱이	chŏn·gaeng·i	scad
다랑어	ta·rang·ŏ	horse mackerel
앤초우비	aen·ch'o·u·bi	anchovy
대하	tae·ha	lobster
정어리	chŏng·ŏ·ri	sardine
뱀장어	paem·jang·ŏ	eel
굴	kul	oyster
게	ke	crab
곤들매기	kon·dŭl·mae·gi	pike
모캐	mo·k'ae	burbot
가자미	ka·ja·mi	turbot/plaice
잉어	ing·ŏ	carp
잔 새우	chan sae·u	shrimp
중(中)새우	chung·sae·u	prawn
연어	yŏn·ŏ	salmon
고등어	ko·dŭng·ŏ	mackerel
가재	ka·jae	crayfish
혀가자미	hyŏ·ga·ja·mi	sole
뱅어	paeng·ŏ	whitebait
농어	nong·ŏ	perch
대구	tae·gu	cod/haddock/whiting
청어	ch'ŏng·ŏ	herring
훈제한 청어	hun·je·han ch'ŏng·ŏ	kipper
대합	tae·hap	clam
넙치	nŏp·ch'i	brill/halibut
성대	sŏng·dae	gurnet
가리비	ka·ri·bi	scallop
숭어	sung·ŏ	mullet
참치	ch'am·ch'i	tunny (tuna)
송어	song·ŏ	trout

Seafood and other specialities

생선회
(saeng·sŏn·hoe)

Sliced fresh, raw fish with soy sauce or red pepper sauce.

매운탕
(mae·un·t'ang)

Hot pepper soup of fish, soybean curd, egg, and vegetables.

삼계탕
(sam·gye·t'ang)

Chicken-ginseng soup. Chicken stuffed with glutinous rice, ginseng, and dried jujubes, steamed and served hot.

만두
(man·du)

Dumplings. Meat, vegetables, and sometimes soybean curd, stuffed into a dumpling and steamed, fried, or boiled in a broth.

모밀 국수
(mo·mil kuk·su)

Buckwheat noodles served with a sweet radish sauce.

냉면
(naeng·myŏn)

Cold potato-flour or buckwheat-flour noodles topped with sliced meat, vegetables, a boiled egg, pepper relish sauce, and ice.

콩 국수
(k'ong kuk·su)

Wheat noodles in fresh soymilk soup.

오뎅 국수
(o·deng kuk·su)

Wheat noodles topped with oriental fishcakes in a broth.

라면
(ra·myŏn)

Instant noodles in instant broth.

우동
(u·dong)

Long, wide wheat noodles with onions, fried soybean curd, red pepper powder, and egg.

비빔밥
(pi·bim·bap)

Rice topped with parboiled fern bracken, bluebell root, soybean sprouts, spinach, and fried egg, mixed with red pepper sauce, to taste. Dried, salted seaweed and a slice or two of sausage are sometimes added.

잡채
(chap·ch'ae)

Mixed vegetables with soybean or rice ver-
micelli. Shredded beef, onions, cucumbers,
carrots, soybean sprouts, mushrooms, and
noodles all seasoned and stir-fried.

신선로
(shin·sŏl·lo)

A regal casserole of vegetables, quail eggs,
strips of meat, fish balls, pine nuts and
gingko nuts mixed together and cooked
over charcoal.

빈대떡
(pin·dae·tŏk)

A pancake made of bean flour and eggs,
filled with strips of pork.

떡국
(tŏk·kuk)

Rice cake soup. Sliced rice cake boiled in
beef soup.

백반
(paek·pan)

Steamed rice. A bowl of rice served with a
variety of *kim·ch'i* (peppery hot fermented
Chinese cabbage, radish and vegetable pickled in salt brine and stored underground in
earthenware jars during the winter),
na·mul (parboiled vegetables) and soybean
paste soup.

Chinese foods

짜장면
(cha·jang·myŏn)

Wheat noodles with pork, seafood, and
vegetable tidbits stir-fried in a sweet-and-
sour black bean sauce.

탕수육
(t'ang·su·yuk)

Deep-fried pork seasoned with sweet-and-
sour vegetables.

Meat

What kind of meat have you got?	어떤 고기가 있습니까?	ŏ·tŏn ko·gi·ga i·ssŭm·ni·ka
I'd like some . . .	…을 주세요.	. . . ŭl chu·se·yo
beef/pork/ veal/mutton	쇠고기/돼지고기/ 송아지고기/양고기	soe·go·gi/twe·ji·go·gi/ song·a·ji·go·gi/yang·go·gi

갈비	kal·bi	T-bone/rib steak
쇠꼬리	soe·ko·ri	oxtail
커틀렛	k'ŏ·t'ŭl·let	escalope
어깻살	ŏ·kae·ssal	shoulder
간	kan	liver
쇠고기	soe·go·gi	beef
목덜미 고기	mok·tŏl·mi ko·gi	neck (best end)
등심 고기	tŭng·shim ko·gi	saddle
송아지 고기	song·a·ji ko·gi	veal
송아지 골	song·a·ji kol	calf's brains
송아지 지라	song·a·ji chi·ra	veal sweetbreads
송아지 로스 고기	song·a·ji ro·sŭ ko·gi	veal cutlets
새끼양 고기	sae·ki·yang ko·gi	lamb
새끼양 갈비	sae·ki·yang kal·bi	lamb chops
소의 허릿고기	so·ŭi hŏ·rit·ko·gi	sirloin
혀	hyŏ	tongue
스튜 고기	sŭ·t'yu ko·gi	stew
샤토브리앙	sya·t'o·bŭ·ri·ang	chateaubriand
콩팥	k'ong·p'at	kidney
스테이크	sŭ·t'e·i·k'ŭ	steak
소시지	so·shi·ji	sausage
투르느도	t'u·rŭ·nŭ·do	tournedos
고기만두	ko·gi·man·du	rissoles
햄	haem	ham
모듬 냉육	mo·dŭm naeng·yuk	cold cuts
비프 스테이크	bi·p'ŭ·sŭ·t'e·i·k'ŭ	beefsteak
돼지 고기	twe·ji ko·gi	pork
돼지 갈비	twe·ji kal·bi	pork chops
베이컨	be·i·k'ŏn	bacon
필레고기	p'il·le·go·gi	fillet
갈비고기	kal·bi·go·gi	chop
커틀렛	k'ŏ·t'ŭl·let	cutlet
양고기	yang·go·gi	mutton

가슴 고기	ka·sŭm ko·gi	breast
내장	nae·jang	tripe
도가니	to·ga·ni	leg
로스트 비프	ro·sŭ·t'ŭ bi·p'ŭ	roast beef
로스트 포크	ro·sŭ·t'ŭ p'o·k'ŭ	roast pork

How do you like your meat?

baked	구운	ku·un
barbecued	바베큐로 한	ba·be·k'yu·ro han
boiled	삶은	sal·mŭn
braised	볶은	po·kŭn
broiled	석쇠에 구운	sŏk·soe·e ku·un
en casserole	오지남비에 지진	o·ji·nam·bi·e chi·jin
fried	프라이한	p'ŭ·ra·i·han
grilled	석쇠에 구운	sŏk·soe·e ku·un
pot-roast	남비에 볶은	nam·bi·e po·kŭn
roast	로스트한	ro·sŭ·t'ŭ·han
stewed	스튜로 한	sŭ·t'yu·ro han
stuffed	속을 넣은	so·gŭl nŏ·ŭn
underdone (rare)	설구운	sŏl·gu·un
medium	보통으로 익힌	po·t'ong·ŭ·ro i·k'in
well-done	잘 익힌	chal i·k'in

EATING OUT

Korean meat dishes

Koreans have developed excellent meat-cooking methods. Beef, pork and chicken are their favorite basics. Of the various meat dishes, *pul·go·gi* is very famous, and popular among foreigners.

We recommend...	···을 잡숴보시지요.	... ŭl chap·swŏ·bo·shi·ji·yo

불고기 (pul·go·gi)	Barbecued beef or pork. Strips of beef or pork marinated in soy sauce, sesame oil, garlic, black pepper, green onions, and toasted sesame seeds that are charcoal-broiled over a grill.
불갈비 (pul·gal·bi)	Barbecued beef or pork ribs. Beef or pork short ribs marinated and barbecued in much the same manner as *pul·go·gi.*
갈비찜 (kal·bi·chim)	Beef rib stew. Short ribs of beef, turnips, chestnuts, and mushrooms marinated, and cooked slowly for a few hours.
설렁탕 (sŏl·lŏng·t'ang)	Rice cooked in a beef and bone stew.
곰창전골 (kop·ch'ang·jŏn·gol)	Tripe casserole. Tripe cooked with mushrooms, onions, garlic, salt, black and red pepper in beef broth with noodles and vegetables added.
닭찜 (tak·chim)	Chicken stew. Chicken stewed with onions, carrots, garlic, black and red pepper, salt or soy sauce, and other spices.
통닭구이 (t'ong·dak·gu·i)	Whole roasted chicken.

Game and poultry

| I'd like some game. | 새고기를 주세요. | sae·go·gi·rŭl chu·se·yo |
| What poultry dishes do you serve? | 무슨 새고기 요리가 있읍니까? | mu·sŭn sae·go·gi yo·ri·ga i·ssŭm·ni·ka |

오리	o·ri	duck
오리새끼	o·ri sae·ki	duckling
오리 스튜	o·ri sŭ·t'yu	duck emincé
오리의 가슴 고기	o·ri·ŭi ka·sŭm ko·gi	duck breast
멧돼지	met·dwe·ji	wild boar
메추리	me·ch'u·ri	quail
거위	kŏ·wi	goose
꿩	kwŏng	pheasant
돼지 새끼	twe·ji sae·ki	suck(l)ing pig
참새	ch'am·sae·	sparrow
닭	tak	chicken
닭의 가슴 고기	ta·gǔi ka·sǔm ko·gi	chicken breast
통닭구이	t'ong·dak·gu·i	roast chicken
비둘기	pi·dul·gi	pigeon
비둘기 새끼	pi·dul·gi sae·ki	squab
칠면조	ch'il·myŏn·jo	turkey
사슴	sa·sŭm	venison escalop

Vegetables and seasonings

What vegetables do you recommend?	무슨 좋은 야채가 있읍니까?	mu·sŭn cho·ŭn ya·ch'ae·ga i·ssŭm·ni·ka
Are they fresh or canned?	신선한 야채입니까, 통조림한 것입니까?	shin·sŏn·han ya·ch'ae·im·ni·ka t'ong·jo·rim·han kŏ·shim·ni·ka
I'd prefer some salad.	나는 샐러드로 하겠읍니다.	na·nŭn sael·lŏ·dŭ·ro ha·ge·ssŭm·ni·da

붉은 양배추	pul·gŭn yang·bae·ch'u	red cabbage
아스파라거스	a·sŭ·p'a·ra·gŏ·sŭ	asparagus
강남콩	kang·nam·k'ong	kidney beans
이집트콩	i·jip·t'ŭ·k'ong	chick peas
완두	wan·du	peas
서양호박	sŏ·yang·ho·bak	marrow (zucchini)
꽃양배추	kot·yang·bae·ch'u	cauliflower
뚱딴지	tung·tan·ji	Jerusalem artichokes
꽃상치	kot·sang·ch'i	endive
양배추	yang·bae·ch'u	cabbage
오이	o·i	cucumber
양갓냉이	yang·gat·naeng·i	watercress
작은 오이	cha·gŭn o·i	gherkins
쌀	ssal	rice
강남콩	kang·nam·k'ong	haricot (French) beans
샐러드	sael·lŏ·dŭ	salad
서양고추냉이	sŏ·yang·go·ch'u·naeng·i	horseradish
감자	kam·ja	potatoes
셀러리	sel·lŏ·ri	celery
잠두	cham·du	broad beans
양파	yang·p'a	onions
사탕무우	sa·t'ang·mu·u	beet (root)
옥수수	ok·su·su	corn on the cob
도마도	to·ma·do	tomatoes
가지	ka·ji	aubergines (eggplant)
당근	tang·gŭn	carrots
마늘	ma·nŭl	garlic
부추	pu·ch'u	leeks
파슬리	p'a·sŭl·li	parsley
피망	p'i·mang	pimiento
버섯	pŏ·sŏt	mushroom

EATING OUT

싹눈 양배추	ssang·nun yang·bae·ch'u	brussels sprouts
사탕옥수수	sa·t'ang·ok·su·su	sweet corn
모듬 야채	mo·dŭm ya·ch'ae	mixed vegetables
무우	mu·u	radishes
상치	sang·ch'i	lettuce
렌즈콩	ren·jŭ·k'ong	lentils

Vegetables may be served:

baked	구운	ku·un
boiled	삶은	sal·mŭn
chopped	썰어 놓은	ssŏ·rŏ no·ŭn
creamed	크림을 친	k'ŭ·ri·mŭl ch'in
diced	네모나게 썬	ne·mo·na·ge ssŏn
fried	프라이한	p'ŭ·ra·i·han
grilled	석쇠에 구운	sŏk·soe·e ku·un
roasted	로스트한	ro·sŭ·t'ŭ·han
stewed	스튜로 한	sŭ·t'yu·ro han
stuffed	속을 넣은	so·gŭl nŏ·ŭn

If you want vegetables to be served in a Western way, you should go to a Western-style or foreign restaurant.

EATING OUT

Fruit

Do you have fresh fruit?	싱싱한 과일이 있읍니까?	shing·shing·han kwa·i·ri i·ssŭm·ni·ka
I'd like a fresh fruit cocktail.	신선한 과일 칵테일을 주세요.	shin·sŏn·han kwa·il k'ak·t'e·i·rŭl chu·se·yo

아몬드	a·mon·dŭ	almonds
살구	sal·gu	apricots
딸기	tal·gi	strawberries
무화과	mu·hwa·gwa	figs
올리브	ol·li·bŭ	olives
오렌지	o·ren·ji	oranges
감	kam	persimmon
나무딸기	na·mu·tal·gi	raspberries
밤	pam	chestnuts
호두	ho·du	walnuts
그레이프프루트	kŭ·re·i·p'ŭ·p'ŭ·ru·t'ŭ	grapefruit
야자 열매	ya·ja yŏl·mae	coconut
버찌	pŏ·chi	cherries
구즈베리	ku·jŭ·be·ri	gooseberries
수박	su·bak	watermelon
배	pae	pear
대추야자 열매	tae·ch'u·ya·ja yŏl·mae	dates
파인애플	p'a·in·ae·p'ŭl	pineapple
개암	kae·am	hazelnuts
바나나	ba·na·na	banana
포도	p'o·do	grapes
서양오얏	sŏ·yang·o·yat	plums
말린 오얏	mal·lin o·yat	prunes
귤	kyul	tangerine
멜론	mel·lon	melon
복숭아	pok·sung·a	peach
사과	sa·gwa	apple
레몬	le·mon	lemon

Dessert

Dessert is foreign to traditional Korean cuisine. Called *di·jŏ·t'ŭ*
in Korean, it was introduced by Westerners about a century
ago. If you've survived all the courses on the menu, you may
want to say:

I'd like a dessert, please.	디저트를 주세요.	di·jŏ·t'ŭ·rŭl chu·se·yo
Something light, please.	뭐 가벼운 걸로 주세요.	mwŏ ka·byŏ·un kŏl·lo chu·se·yo
Just a small portion.	아주 조금만 주세요.	a·ju cho·gŭm·man chu·se·yo
Nothing more, thanks.	이제 됐읍니다.	i·je twe·ssŭm·ni·da

If you're not sure what to order, ask the waiter:

What do you have for dessert?	디저트는 무엇이 있읍니까?	di·jŏ·t'ŭ·nŭn mu·ŏ·shi i·ssŭm·ni·ka
What do you recommend?	무엇이 좋습니까?	mu·ŏ·shi cho·ssŭm·ni·ka

아몬드 수플레	a·mon·dŭ su·p'ŭl·le	almond soufflé
아이스크림	a·i·sŭ·k'ŭ·rim	ice-cream
아이스크림 커피	a·i·sŭ·k'ŭ·rim k'ŏ·p'i	coffee ice-cream
사과 파이	sa·gwa p'a·i	apple pie
단 오믈렛	tan o·mŭl·let	sweet omelet
거품이 일게 한 크림	kŏ·p'um·i il·ge han k'ŭ·rim	whipped cream
나무딸기 아이스크림	na·mu·tal·gi a·i·sŭ·k'ŭ·rim	raspberry ice-cream
나무딸기 수플레	na·mu·tal·gi su·p'ŭl·le	frozen raspberry soufflé
케이크	k'e·i·k'ŭ	cake
커피 케이크	k'ŏ·p'i k'e·i·k'ŭ	coffee cake
수플레	su·p'ŭl·le	soufflé
딸기 아이스크림	tal·gi a·i·sŭ·k'ŭ·rim	strawberry sundae
초콜렛 케이크	ch'o·k'ol·let k'e·i·k'ŭ	chocolate cake
초콜렛 아이스크림	ch'o·k'ol·let a·i·sŭ·k'ŭ·rim	chocolate sundae
초콜렛 푸딩	ch'o·k'ol·let p'u·ding	chocolate pudding
붉은 포도주에 조린 배	pul·gŭn p'o·do·ju·e cho·rin pae	pears baked in red wine

크림을 넣고 조린 배	k'ŭ·rim·ŭl nŏ·k'o cho·rin pae	pears cooked with cream
버찌 브랜디에 담근 파인 애플	pŏ·chi pŭ·raen·di·e tam·gŭn p'a·in·ae·p'ŭl	pineapple with kirsch (cherry brandy)
바나나 튀김	ba·na·na t'wi·gim	banana fritters
바나나 플람베	ba·na·na p'ŭl·lam·be	banana flambé
피치 멜바	p'i·ch'i mel·ba	peach melba
푸딩	p'u·ding	pudding
프루트 칵테일	p'ŭ·ru·t'ŭ k'ak·t'e·il	fruit cocktail
럼을 넣은 오믈렛	rŏm·ŭl nŏ·ŭn o·mŭl·let	rum omelet
레몬 아이스크림	le·mon a·i·sŭ·k'ŭ·rim	lemon ice-cream
레몬 수플레	le·mon su·p'ŭl·le	lemon soufflé

That's the end of our menu. For drinks, see page 60. But after the feast comes. . .

The bill (check)

May I have the bill (check), please?	계산서 주시겠어요?	kye·san·sŏ chu·shi·ge·ssŏ·yo
Isn't there a mistake?	틀리지는 않았읍니까?	t'ŭl·li·ji·nŭn a·na·ssŭm·ni·ka
Is service included?	서비스료도 들어 있읍니까?	sŏ·bi·sŭ·ryo·do tŭ·rŏ i·ssŭm·ni·ka
Is the cover charge included?	테이블 챠지도 들어 있읍니까?	t'e·i·bŭl ch'ya·ji·do tŭ·rŏ i·ssŭm·ni·ka
Do you accept traveller's cheques?	여행자 수표도 받읍니까?	yŏ·haeng·ja su·p'yo·do pa·ssŭm·ni·ka
Thank you, this is for you.	고맙습니다, 이건 팁입니다.	ko·map·sŭm·ni·da i·gŏn t'i·bim·ni·da
Keep the change.	거스름돈은 가지세요.	kŏ·sŭ·rŭm·don·ŭn ka·ji·se·yo

서비스료 포함
SERVICE INCLUDED

| That was a very good meal. We enjoyed it. | 아주 맛있었읍니다. 잘 먹었읍니다. | a·ju ma·shi·ssŏ·ssŭm·ni·da chal mŏ·gŏ·ssŭm·ni·da |
| We'll come again some time. | 언제고 또 오겠읍니다. | ŏn·je·go to o·ge·ssŭm·ni·da |

Complaints

But perhaps you'll have something to complain about. . .

There's a draught here. Could you give us another table?	여기는 바람이 들어옵니다. 다른 테이블을 줄 수 있어요?	yŏ·gi·nŭn pa·ram·i dŭ·rŏ·om·ni·da.ta·rŭn t'e·i·bŭ·rŭl chul·su i·ssŏ·yo
That's not what I ordered. I asked for. . .	이건 내가 주문한 것이 아니에요. 난 …을 주문 했어요.	i·gŏn nae·ga chu·mun·han kŏ·shi a·ni·e·yo. nan ...ŭl chu·mun·hae·ssŏ·yo
I don't like this/I can't eat this.	이건 좋아 안합니다/이 건 먹을 수가 없어요.	i·gŏn cho·a an·ham·ni·da/i·gŏn mŏ·gŭl su·ga ŏp·sŏ·yo
May I change this?	이걸 바꾸어 주시겠어요?	i·gŏl pa·ku·ŏ chu·shi·ge·ssŏ·yo
The meat is. . .	이 고기는…	i ko·gi·nŭn. . .
overdone	너무 익었읍니다	nŏ·mu i·gŏ·ssŭm·ni·da
underdone	덜 익었읍니다	tŏl i·gŏ·ssŭm·ni·da
too rare	너무 날것입니다	nŏ·mu nal·gŏ·shim·ni·da
too tough	너무 질깁니다	nŏ·mu chil·gim·ni·da
This is too. . .	이것은…	i·gŏ·sŭn. . .
bitter/salty/sweet	너무 씁니다/잡니다/답니다	nŏ·mu ssŭm·ni·da/cham·ni·da/tam·ni·da
The food is cold.	이 음식은 차요.	i ŭm·shi·gŭn ch'a·yo
This is not fresh.	이것은 신선하지 않군요.	i·gŏ·sŭn shin·sŏn·ha·ji an·kun·yo
Would you ask the head waiter to come over?	급사장에게 오라고 해주 겠어요?	kŭp·sa·jang·e·ge o·ra·go hae·ju·ge·ssŏ·yo

Drinks

Beer

There are two brands of popular Korean-brewed beers: *OB*
and *Crown*. There are also several available that are brewed
under licence: *Heineken* and *Budweiser*.

| I'd like a (cold) beer, please. | (찬) 맥주를 주세요. | (ch'an) maek·chu·rŭl chu·se·yo |

So·ju

A strong colourless spirit distilled from grains, this popular
alcoholic beverage is enjoyed along with such dishes as bar-
becued pork and hot peppery fish soup, providing a most convi-
ial atmosphere at little cost.

If you would like to taste it, say:

| May I have a cup of so·ju please? | 소주 한 잔 주세요. | so·ju han chan chu·se·yo |

Wine

Introduced from abroad only a comparatively short time ago,
wine production does not have a very long history in Korea.
Many interesting labels, however, are now available here. The
Oriental Brewery Co. produces a Riesling under the label
"Majuang" that is a favorite at better-class restaurants every-
where. Rosé and red wines are also produced. In addition,
the Jinro Corp. has recently produced a new brand of wine
called *Château Montblé*. Aside from these, many other wines
are also available.

I'd like ... of ...	···을 ···주세요.	... ŭl ... chu·se·yo
a bottle	한 병	han pyŏng
half a bottle	반 병	pan pyŏng
a glass	한 잔	han chan
a litre	1 리터	il ri·t'ŏ
I want a bottle of white wine.	백포도주를 한 병 주세요.	paek p'o·do·ju·rŭl han pyŏng chu·se·yo
How much is a bottle of ... ?	···은 한 병에 얼마입니까?	... ŭn han pyŏng·e ŏl·ma·im·ni·ka
That's too expensive.	너무 비싸군요.	nŏ·mu pi·ssa·gun·yo
Haven't you anything cheaper?	더 싼 것은 없습니까?	tŏ ssan gŏ·sŭn ŏp·sŭm·ni·ka
Fine, that will do.	좋습니다, 그것으로 됐어요.	cho·ssŭm·ni·da ku·gŏ·sŭ·ro twe·ssŏ·yo

If you enjoyed the wine, you may want to say:

Bring me another ..., please.	···을 더 갖다 주세요.	... ŭl tŏ kat·ta chu·se·yo
glass/bottle	한 잔/한 병	han chan/han pyŏng
What's the name of this wine?	이 포도주 이름이 무엇입니까?	i p'o·do·ju i·rŭm·i mu·ŏ·shim·ni·ka
Where does this wine come from?	이 포도주는 어디 포도주입니까?	i p'o·do·ju·nŭn ŏ·di p'o·do·ju·im·ni·ka
How old is this wine?	이 포도주는 몇년 됐나요?	i p'o·do·ju·nŭn myŏt·nyŏn twen·na·yo

dry	드라이	dŭ·ra·i
red	붉은	pul·gŭn
rosé	로제	ro·je
sparkling	거품이 나는	kŏ·p'um·i na·nŭn
sweet	단	tan
white	흰	hŭin
chilled	차게 한	ch'a·ge han
at room temperature	실내 온도와 같은	sil·lae on·do·wa ka·t'ŭn

Other alcoholic drinks

Perhaps you would like to order one of the following drinks:

aperitif	반주	pan·ju
beer	맥주	maek·chu
brandy	브랜디	bǔ·raen·di
cider	사이다	sa·i·da
cognac	코냑	k'o·nyak
gin	진	chin
gin fizz	진 피즈	chin p'i·jǔ
gin and tonic	진 토닉	chin t'o·nik
liqueur	리큐르	li·k'yu·rǔ
port	포트와인	p'o·tǔ·wa·in
rum	럼	rǒm
sherry	셰리	sye·ri
vermouth	베르못	pe·rǔ·mut
vodka	보드카	po·dǔ·k'a
screwdriver	스크루드라이버	sǔ·k'ǔ·ru·dǔ·ra·i·bǒ
whisky	위스키	wi·sǔ·k'i
neat (straight)/on the rocks	스트레이트/온 더 락	sǔ·t'ǔ·re·i·t'ǔ/on tǒ rak
whisky and soda	하이볼	ha·i·bol

glass	한 잔	han chan
bottle	한 병	han pyǒng
single	싱글	sing·gǔl
double	더블	dǒ·bǔl

Korea imports a lot of whisky, but it's worth trying a few of its home-produced blends. Some of the best-known brands are *Valley 9*, *VIP*, and *Gilbert*. Others, such as *Passport* and *Blackstone*, are made under licence.

I'd like to taste Valley 9, please.	베리나인을 맛보고 싶은 데요.	pe·ri·na·in·ǔl mat·bo·go shi·p'ǔn·de·yo
Bring me ... of ..., please.	⋯을 ⋯ 갖다 주세요.	...ǔl ...kat·ta chu·se·yo

EATING OUT

```
┌─────────────────┐
│      건 배       │
│   (kŏn·bae)     │
│     CHEERS!     │
└─────────────────┘
```

Other beverages

I'd like a ...	···을 주세요.	. . . ŭl chu·se·yo
Have you any ... ?	···이 있읍니까?	. . . i i·ssŭm·ni·ka
chocolate	초콜렛	ch'o·k'ol·let
Coca-Cola	코카콜라	k'o·k'a·k'ol·la
coffee	커피	k'ŏ·p'i
cup of coffee	커피 한 잔	k'ŏ·p'i han chan
coffee with cream	크림을 탄 커피	k'ŭ·rim·ŭl t'an k'ŏ·p'i
espresso coffee	에스프레소 커피	e·sŭ·p'ŭ·re·so k'ŏ·p'i
iced coffee	아이스 커피	a·i·sŭ k'ŏ·p'i
fruit juice	프루트 쥬스	p'ŭ·ru·t'ŭ chyu·sŭ
grapefruit	그레이프프루트	gŭ·re·i·p'ŭ·p'ŭ·ru·t'ŭ
lemon/orange	레몬/오렌지	le·mon/o·ren·ji
pineapple/tomato	파인애플/도마도	p'a·in·ae·p'ŭl/to·ma·do
lemonade	레모네이드	re·mo·ne·i·dŭ
fizzy/still	거품을 일게 한/거품이 안 나는	kŏ·p'um·ŭl il·ge han/kŏ·p'um·i an na·nŭn
milk	우유	u·yu
milk shake	밀크 셰이크	mil·k'ŭ sye·i·k'ŭ
mineral water	미네랄 워터	mi·ne·ral wŏ·t'ŏ
orangeade	오렌지에이드	o·ren·ji·e·i·dŭ
Pepsi-Cola	펩시콜라	p'ep·shi·k'ol·la
soda water	소다수	so·da·su
tea	홍차	hong·ch'a
with milk/lemon	우유를 탄/레몬을 탄	u·yu·rŭl t'an/le·mon·ŭl t'an
tonic water	토닉 워터	t'o·nik wŏ·t'ŏ

Eating light — Snacks

I'll have one of these, please.	이것을 하나 주십시오.	i·gŏ·sŭl ha·na chu·ship·shi·yo
Give me two of these and one of those.	이것 두 개 하고 저것 한 개를 주세요.	i·gŏt tu·gae ha·go chŏ·gŏ han·gae·rŭl chu·se·yo
to the left	왼쪽의	oen·cho·gŭi
to the right	오른쪽의	o·rŭn·cho·gŭi
above	위의	wi·ŭi
below	아래의	a·rae·ŭi
Give me a/an/some . . . , please.	…을 주세요.	. . . ŭl chu·se·yo
beefburger	비프버거	bi·p'ŭ·bŏ·gŏ
biscuits	비스킷	bi·sŭ·k'it
bread	빵	pang
butter	버터	bŏ·t'ŏ
cake	케이크	k'e·i·k'ŭ
candy	캔디	k'aen·di
chocolate (bar)	(막대) 초콜렛	(mak·tae) ch'o·k'ol·let
cookies	쿠키	k'u·k'i
hamburger	햄버거	haem·bŏ·gŏ
hot dog	핫도그	hat·do·gŭ
ice-cream	아이스크림	a·i·sŭ·k'ŭ·rim
pastry	과자	kwa·ja
pie	파이	p'a·i
roll	로울빵	ro·ul·pang
salad	샐러드	sael·lŏ·dŭ
sandwich	샌드위치	saen·dŭ·wi·ch'i
sweets	사탕	sa·t'ang
toast	토스트	t'o·sŭ·t'ŭ
waffles	와플	wa·p'ŭl
How much is it?	그것은 얼마입니까 ?	kŭ·gŏ·sŭn ŏl·ma·im·ni·ka

Travelling around

Plane

Korea has two domestic airlines, Korean Air and Asiana, which serve most of the larger cities.

Do you speak English?	영어를 할 줄 아십니까?	yŏng·ŏ·rŭl hal·chul a·shim·ni·ka
Is there a flight to Cheju Island?	제주도행 비행기가 있읍니까?	che·ju·do·haeng pi·haeng·gi·ga i·ssŭm·ni·ka
When's the next plane to Cheju Island?	다음의 제주도행 비행기는 몇시에 있읍니까?	ta·ŭm·ŭi che·ju·do·haeng pi·haeng·gi·nŭn myŏt·shi·e i·ssŭm·ni·ka
Can I make a connection to Pusan?	부산행으로 연결될 수 있읍니까?	pu·san·haeng·ŭ·ro yŏn·gyŏl·toel su i·ssŭm·ni·ka
I'd like a ticket to New York.	뉴욕행 표를 한 장 주세요.	nyu·yok·haeng p'yo·rŭl han chang chu·se·yo
What's the fare to Bangkok?	방콕까지 요금이 얼마입니까?	bang·k'ok·ka·ji yo·gŭm·i ŏl·ma·im·ni·ka
single (one-way)	편도	p'yŏn·do
return (roundtrip)	왕복	wang·bok
What time does the plane take off?	비행기는 몇시에 이륙합니까?	pi·haeng·gi·nŭn myŏt·shi·e i·ryuk·ham·ni·ka
What time do I have to check in?	몇시에 체크인해야 합니까?	myŏt·shi·e ch'e·k'ŭ·in·hae·ya ham·ni·ka
What's the flight number?	플라이트 번호는 몇번입니까?	p'ŭl·la·i·t'ŭ pŏn·ho·nŭn myŏt·pŏn·im·ni·ka
What time do we arrive?	몇시에 도착합니까?	myŏt·shi·e to·ch'ak·ham·ni·ka

도착 ARRIVAL	출발 DEPARTURE

Train

If you're worried about train tickets, times of departure etc., go to a travel agency(*yŏ·haeng·sa*) where they speak English or ask at your hotel.

Train travel in Korea is fast and punctual on the main lines. First-class (green) coaches are comfortable with reclining seats. To board green-car coaches, you'll have to buy a green-car ticket in addition to an ordinary ticket. Second-class coaches are often crowded.

All station names and important signs are printed in English.

Types of trains

Four kinds of train service are available in Korea. The types of trains in order of increasing speed, comfort, and punctuality are:

비둘기호 (pi·dul·gi·ho)	Stops at each station along the way.
통일호 (t'ong·il·ho)	Limited express, reserved seats available, occasionally with dining car.
무궁화호 (mu·gung·hwa·ho)	Express, air-conditioned.
새마을호 (sae·ma·ŭl·ho)	Luxury, air-conditioned super-express with dining car.

It is wise to purchase tickets in advance, especially during holidays and summer vacation months.

To the railway station

Where's the railway station?	철도역이 어디입니까?	ch'ŏl·to·yŏ·gi ŏ·di·im·ni·ka
Taxi, please!	택시를 부탁합니다.	t'aek·shi·rŭl pu·t'ak·ham·ni·da
Take me to the railway station.	역까지 태워다 주세요.	yŏk·ka·ji t'ae·wŏ·da chu·se·yo
What's the fare?	요금이 얼마입니까?	yo·gŭm·i ŏl·ma·im·ni·ka

Tickets

Where's the ... ?	…이 어디입니까?	... i ŏ·di·im·ni·ka
information office	안내소	an·nae·so
reservation office	예약 접수처	ye·yak chŏp·su·ch'ŏ
ticket office	매표소	mae·p'yo·so
I want a ticket to Kyŏngju, second-class.	경주행 2등표 한 장 부탁합니다.	kyŏng·ju·haeng i·dŭng·p'yo han chang pu·t'ak·ham·ni·da
I'd like two tickets to Taegu.	대구까지 두 장 주세요.	tae·gu·ka·ji tu chang chu·se·yo
How much is the fare to Kangnŭng?	강릉까지 요금이 얼마입니까?	kang·nŭng·ka·ji yo·gŭm·i ŏl·ma·im·ni·ka
Is it half price for a child? He is thirteen.	아이들은 반액입니까? 그 애는 열 세살인데요.	a·i·dŭl·ŭn pan·aek·im·ni·ka? kŭ ae·nŭn yŏl·se·sal·in·de·yo

Note: Children up to the age of 6 travel free. From 6 to 12 year olds pay half fare.

Possible answers

1등입니까, 2등입니까?	First or second class?
12 세까지는 반액입니다.	It's half price up to the age of 12.
대인요금을 내야 합니다.	You'll have to pay full fare.

FOR TAXI, see page 27

TRAVELLING AROUND

Further enquiries

Is it a through train?	그것은 직행 열차입니까?	kŭ·gŏ·sŭn chik·t'ong yŏl·ch'a·im·ni·ka
Does this train stop at Suwŏn?	이 열차는 수원에 섭니까?	i yŏl·ch'a·nŭn su·wŏn·e sŏm·ni·ka
When is the ... train to Pusan?	부산행 …열차는 몇시에 있읍니까?	pu·san·haeng ... yŏl·ch'a·nŭn myŏt·shi·e i·ssŭm·ni·ka
first/last/next	첫/마지막/다음	ch'ŏt/ma·ji·mak/ta·ŭm
What time does the train from Kwangju arrive?	광주에서 오는 열차는 몇시에 도착합니까?	kwang·ju·e·sŏ o·nŭn yŏl·ch'a·nŭn myŏt·shi·e to·ch'ak·ham·ni·ka
What time does the train for Kangnŭng leave?	강릉행 열차는 몇시에 출발니까?	kang·nŭng·haeng yŏl·ch'a·nŭn myŏt·shi·e ch'ul·bal·ham·ni·ka
Is the train late?	열차가 지연됩니까?	yŏl·ch'a·ga chi·yŏn·doem·ni·ka
Is there a dining car on the train?	그 열차에 식당차가 있읍니까?	kŭ yŏl·ch'a·e shik·tang·ch'a·ga i·ssŭm·ni·ka

입구	ENTRANCE
출구	EXIT
승강장	TO THE PLATFORMS

Where's the ... ?

Where's the ... ?	…은 어디입니까?	... ŭn ŏ·di·im·ni·ka
bar	주점	chu·jŏm
buffet	부페	bu·p'e
left-luggage office (baggage check)	수하물 보관소	su·ha·mul po·gwan·so
lost property (lost-and-found) office	분실물 취급소	pun·shil·mul ch'wi·gŭp·so
newsstand	신문판매대	shin·mun p'an·mae·dae
restaurant	식당	shik·tang
waiting room	대합실	tae·hap·shil
Where are the toilets?	화장실은 어디입니까?	hwa·jang·shi·rŭn ŏ·di·im·ni·ka

Platform (track)

What track does the train for Pusan leave from?	부산행 열차는 몇번 선에서 출발합니까?	pu·san·haeng yŏl·ch'a·nŭn myŏt·pŏn sŏn·e·sŏ ch'ul·bal·ham·ni·ka
What track does the train from Pusan arrive at?	부산에서 오는 열차는 몇번 선에 도착합니까?	pu·san·e·sŏ o·nŭn yŏl·ch'a·nŭn myŏt·pŏn sŏn·e to·ch'ak·ham·ni·ka
Where is platform 7?	7번 선은 어디입니까?	7·bŏn sŏn·ŭn ŏ·di·im·ni·ka
Is this the right platform for the train to ...?	...행 열차는 여기서 탑니까?	... haeng yŏl·ch'a·nŭn yŏ·gi·sŏ t'am·ni·ka

Possible answers

그것은 직행 열차입니다.	It's a direct train.
...에서 바꿔 타셔야 합니다.	You have to change at ...
...에서 보통 열차로 바꿔 타세요.	Change at ... and get a local train.
...번 선은 ...입니다.	Platform ... is ...
저기/아래층	over there/downstairs
왼쪽/오른쪽	on the left/on the right
...행 열차는 ...시 ...분에 ...번 선에서 출발합니다.	The train to ... will leave at ... from platform ...
...행 ...열차는 ...분 지연될 예정입니다.	The ... train for ... will be ... minutes late.
...에서 오는 열차가 ...번 선에 도착됩니다.	The train from ... is now arriving at platform ...
...분 지연될 예정입니다.	There'll be a delay of ... minutes.

All aboard . . .

Excuse me. May I get past?	실례합니다. 지나가도 됩니까?	shil·lye·ham·ni·da chi·na·ga·do toem·ni·ka
Is this seat taken?	이 자리에 사람이 있읍니까?	i cha·ri·e sa·ram·i i·ssüm·ni·ka

금 연
NO SMOKING

I think that's my seat.	그 자리는 내 자리 같은데요.	kŭ cha·ri·nŭn nae cha·ri ka·t'ŭn·de·yo
What station is this?	여기는 어디 역입니까?	yŏ·gi·nŭn ŏ·di yŏ·gim·ni·ka
How long does the train stop here?	여기서 얼마나 정차합니까?	yŏ·gi·sŏ ŏl·ma·na chŏng·ch'a·ham·ni·ka
Can you tell me at what time we get to Pusan?	부산에 몇시에 도착하는지 가르쳐 주시겠어요?	pu·san·e myŏt·shi·e to·ch'ak·ha·nŭn·ji ka·rŭ·ch'yŏ chu·shi·ge·ssŏ·yo
When do we get to Kyŏngju?	경주에는 몇시에 도착합니까?	kyŏng·ju·e·nŭn myŏt·shi·e to·ch'ak·ham·ni·ka

Sometime on the journey the ticket-inspector (*ch'a·jang*) will come around and say: *Ch'a·p'yo chom po·yŏ chu·se·yo* (Tickets, please).

Eating

You can get snacks and drinks in the buffet car and in the dining car when it isn't being used for main meals. On express trains, waitresses come around with sweets, snacks and drinks. They also sell *to·shi·rak* (station lunch) containing a typical Korean lunch (boiled rice, beans boiled in soysauce, cooked egg, fish, seasoned vegetables, etc.). This box lunch can also be bought at the stations during the train's stop.

Sleeping

Are there any free compartments in the sleeping-car?	침대차에 빈 칸이 있읍니까?	ch'im·dae·ch'a·e pin k'an·i i·ssŭm·ni·ka
Where's the sleeping-car?	침대차가 어디입니까?	ch'im·dae·ch'a·ga ŏ·di·im·ni·ka
Compartments 18 and 19, please.	18번 칸과 19번 칸을 안내해 주세요.	18 bŏn k'an·gwa 19 bŏn k'an·ŭl an·nae·hae chu·se·yo
Would you make up our berths?	침대를 준비해 주시겠어요?	ch'im·dae·rŭl chun·bi·hae chu·shi·ge·ssŏ·yo
Would you call me at 7 o'clock?	7시에 깨워 주시겠어요?	7 shi·e kae·wŏ chu·shi·ge·ssŏ·yo
Would you bring me some coffee in the morning?	아침에 커피를 좀 갖다 주시겠어요?	a·ch'im·e k'ŏ·p'i·rŭl chom kat·ta chu·shi·ge·ssŏ·yo

Baggage and porters

Can you help me with my bags?	내 짐을 운반해 줄 수 있읍니까?	nae chim·ŭl un·ban·hae chul·su i·ssŭm·ni·ka
Put them down here, please.	그것을 여기에 내려놔 주세요.	kŭ·gŏ·sŭl yŏ·gi·e nae·ryŏ·nwa chu·se·yo

Lost !

We hope you'll have no need for the following phrases during your trip... but just in case:

Where's the lost property (lost-and-found) office?	분실물 취급소는 어디입니까?	pun·shil·mul ch'wi·gŭp·so·nŭn ŏ·di·im·ni·ka
I've lost my...	…을 잃어버렸어요.	...ŭl i·rŏ·bŏ·ryŏ·ssŏ·yo
I lost it in...	…에서 잃어버렸어요.	...e·sŏ i·rŏ·bŏ·ryŏ·ssŏ·yo
It's very valuable.	그건 매우 중요한 것입니다.	kŭ·gŏn mae·u chung·yo·han kŏ·shim·ni·da

FOR PORTERS, also see page 24

TRAVELLING AROUND

Timetables

If you intend to do a lot of train travel, it might be a good idea to buy a timetable. A condensed English-language timetable is available free of charge from the Korean National Railway, travel agencies or the tourist information office.

I'd like a timetable, please.	시간표를 하나 주세요.	shi·gan·p'yo·rǔl ha·na chu·se·yo

Underground (subway)

The *chi·ha·ch'ŏl* in Seoul corresponds to the London underground or the New York subway. The lines extend from the centre to the outer suburbs. A map showing the various lines and stations is displayed outside every station. Pocket maps can be obtained at any station from the ticket office or at newsstands and travel agencies.

Fares depend on distance. If you'd like to use the *chi·ha·ch'ŏl* regularly, it's a good idea to get a book of tickets (*hoe·su·gwŏn*). This will mean a small saving on fares.

It may be better not to use the underground during rush hours, as the trains can get extremely crowded.

Bus

In most cases, a bus token or ticket should be purchased at a kiosk before boarding your bus. You can buy a book of tickets (*hoe-su-gwŏn*) for multiple journeys.

I'd like a book of tickets.	회수권을 한 권 주세요.	hoe·su·gwŏn·ŭl han kwŏn chu·se·yo
Where can I get a bus to...?	…행 버스는 어디서 탑니까?	...haeng bŏ·su·nŭn ŏ·di·sŏ t'am·ni·ka
What bus do I take for...?	…행 버스는 어느 것입니까?	...haeng bŏ·su·nŭn ŏ·nŭ kŏ·shim·ni·ka
Where's the...?	…은 어디입니까?	... ŭn ŏ·di·im·ni·ka
bus stop	버스 정류장	bŏ·su chŏng·ryu·jang
terminal	종점	chong·jŏm
When is the ... bus to...?	…행의 …버스는 언제 있읍니까?	...haeng·ŭi ... bŏ·su·nŭn ŏn·je i·ssŭm·ni·ka
first/last/next	첫/마지막/다음	ch'ŏt/ma·ji·mak/ta·ŭm
How often do the buses to ... run?	…행의 버스는 몇분마다 있읍니까?	...haeng·ŭi bŏ·su·nŭn myŏt·pun ma·da i·ssŭm·ni·ka
How much is the fare to...?	…까지의 요금은 얼마입니까?	... ka·ji·ŭi yo·gŭm·ŭn ŏl·ma·im·ni·ka
Do I have to change buses?	버스를 갈아타야 합니까?	bŏ·su·rŭl ka·ra·t'a·ya ham·ni·ka
How long does the journey take?	시간이 얼마나 걸립니까?	shi·gan·i ŏl·ma·na kŏl·lim·ni·ka
Will you tell me when to get off?	언제 내리면 좋은지 일러 주시겠어요?	ŏn·je nae·ri·myŏn cho·ŭn·ji il·lŏ chu·shi·ge·ssŏ·yo
I want to get off at...	…에서 내리고 싶은데요.	...e·sŏ nae·ri·go shi·p'ŭn·de·yo
Please let me off at the next stop.	다음 정류장에서 내려 주세요.	ta·ŭm chŏng·ryu·jang·e·sŏ nae·ryŏ chu·se·yo
May I have my luggage, please?	제 짐을 주시겠어요?	che chim·ŭl chu·shi·ge·ssŏ·yo

---

버스 정류장   BUS STOP

Or try one of these to get around:

bicycle	자전거	cha·jŏn·gŏ
boat	보트	bo·t'ŭ
motorboat	모터보트	mo·t'ŏ·bo·t'ŭ
rowboat	노로 젓는 보트	no·ro chŏt·nŭn bo·t'ŭ
sailboat	요트	yo·t'ŭ
helicopter	헬리콥터	hel·li·k'op·t'ŏ
hitchhiking	히치하이킹	hi·ch'i·ha·i·k'ing
horse-back riding	승마	sŭng·ma
hovercraft	호버크래프트	ho·bŏ·k'ŭ·rae·p'ŭ·t'ŭ
motorcycle	오토바이	o·t'o·ba·i

and if you're really stuck, just. . .

walk	걷다	kŏt·ta

Around and about—Sightseeing

Here we're more concerned with the cultural aspects of life than with entertainment; and, for the moment, with towns rather than the countryside. If you want a guide book, ask ...

Can you recommend a good guide book for ...?	…의 좋은 안내서를 가르쳐 주시겠어요?	... ŭi cho·ŭn an·nae·sŏ·rŭl ka·rŭ·ch'yŏ chu·shi·ge·ssŏ·yo
Is there a tourist office?	여행 안내소가 있읍니까?	yŏ·haeng an·nae·so·ga i·ssŭm·ni·ka
Where's the tourist information centre?	관광 안내소는 어디에 있읍니까?	kwan·gwang an·nae·so·nŭn ŏ·di·e i·ssŭm·ni·ka
What are the main points of interest?	특히 재미있는 것은 무엇입니까?	t'ŭk·hi chae·mi·in·nŭn kŏ·sŭn mu·ŏ·shim·ni·ka
We're only here for ...	여기에는 …밖에 있지 않습니다.	yŏ·gi·e·nŭn ... pa·ke it·chi an·sŭm·ni·da
a few hours	2, 3시간	i·sam·shi·gan
a day	하루	ha·ru
three days	3일	sam·il
a week	1주일	il·chu·il
Can you recommend a sightseeing tour?	관광 코스를 가르쳐 주시겠어요?	kwan·gwang k'o·sŭ·rŭl ka·rŭ·ch'yŏ chu·shi·ge·ssŏ·yo
Where does the bus start from?	버스는 어디서 출발합니까?	bŏ·sŭ·nŭn ŏ·di·sŏ ch'ul·bal·ham·ni·ka
Will it pick us up at the hotel?	호텔에 데리러 옵니까?	ho·t'el·e te·ri·rŏ om·ni·ka
What bus/train do we want?	어느 버스/기차에 탑니까?	ŏ·nŭ bŏ·sŭ/ki·ch'a·e t'am·ni·ka
How much does the tour cost?	그 관광 여행은 비용이 얼마입니까?	kŭ kwan·gwang yŏ·haeng·ŭn pi·yong·i ŏl·ma·im·ni·ka
What time does the tour start?	그 관광은 몇시에 출발합니까?	kŭ kwan·gwang·ŭn myŏt·shi·e ch'ul·bal·ham·ni·ka
We'd like to rent a car for the day.	차를 하루 빌리고 싶은데요.	ch'a·rŭl ha·ru pil·li·go shi·p'ŭn·de·yo

FOR TIME OF DAY, see page 178

SIGHTSEEING

| Is there an English-speaking guide? | 영어를 할 줄 아는 안내원이 있읍니까? | yŏng·ŏ·rŭl hal·chul a·nŭn an·nae·wŏn·i i·ssŭm·ni·ka |
| Where's the.../ Where are the ...? | …은 어디입니까? | ... ŭn ŏ·di·im·ni·ka |

abbey	수도원	su·do·wŏn
aquarium	수족관	su·jok·kwan
arch	아치	a·ch'i
botanical gardens	식물원	shik·mul·wŏn
building	건물	kŏn·mul
castle	성	sŏng
cathedral	대성당	tae·sŏng·dang
cave	동굴	tong·gul
cemetery	묘지	myo·ji
church	교회	kyo·hoe
convent	수녀원	su·nyŏ·wŏn
convention hall	음악회장	ŭm·ak·hoe·jang
docks	부두	pu·du
downtown area	시내	shi·nae
exhibition	전람회	chŏl·lam·hoe
factory	공장	kong·jang
fair	시장	shi·jang
fortress	성채	sŏng·ch'ae
fountain	샘	saem
gardens	정원	chŏng·wŏn
gate	성문	sŏng·mun
grotto	석굴	sŏk·kul
harbour	항구	hang·gu
lake	호수	ho·su
law courts	법원	pŏp·wŏn
library	도서관	to·sŏ·gwan
market	시장	shi·jang
monastery	수도원	su·do·wŏn
monument	기념비	ki·nyŏm·bi
museum	박물관	pang·mul·gwan
observatory	천문대	ch'ŏn·mun·dae
old town	옛 마을	yen·ma·ŭl
pagoda	탑	t'ap
palace	궁전	kung·jŏn
park	공원	kong·wŏn
planetarium	천문관	ch'ŏn·mun·gwan

shopping centre	쇼핑 센터	syo·p'ing sen·t'ŏ
shrine	사당	sa·dang
square	광장	kwang·jang
stadium	경기장	kyŏng·gi·jang
statue	(동)상	(tong) sang
stock exchange	증권거래소	chŭng·gwŏn·gŏ·rae·so
street	거리	kŏ·ri
television studios	텔레비 스튜디오	t'el·le·bi sŭ·t'yu·di·o
temple	절	chŏl
tomb	무덤	mu·dŏm
tower	탑	t'ap
town centre	중심가	chung·shim·ga
town hall	시청	shi·ch'ŏng
university	대학	tae·hak
zoo	동물원	tong·mul·wŏn

Admission

Is the ... open on Sundays?	...은 일요일에도 문을 엽니까?	... ŭn il·yo·il·e·do mun·ŭl yŏm·ni·ka
When does it open?	몇시에 문을 엽니까?	myŏt·shi·e mun·ŭl yŏm·ni·ka
When does it close?	몇시에 문을 닫습니까?	myŏt·shi·e mun·ŭl ta·ssŭm·ni·ka
How much is the admission charge?	입장료는 얼마입니까?	ip·chang·nyo·nŭn ŏl·ma·im·ni·ka
Is there any reduction for ...?	...에게 할인이 있읍니까?	... e·ge ha·rin·i i·ssŭm·ni·ka
students/children	학생/어린이	hak·saeng/ŏ·ri·ni
Have you a guide book (in English)?	(영어로 된) 안내서가 있읍니까?	(yŏng·ŏ·ro toen) an·nae·sŏ·ga i·ssŭm·ni·ka
Can I buy a catalogue?	카탈로그를 구입할 수 있을까요?	k'a·t'al·lo·gŭ·rŭl ku·ip·hal su i·ssŭl·ka·yo
Is it all right to take pictures?	사진을 찍어도 괜찮습니까?	sa·jin·ŭl chi·gŏ·do kwen·ch'an·sŭm·ni·ka

무료 입장	ADMISSION FREE
사진촬영금지	NO CAMERAS ALLOWED

Who—What—When ?

What's that building ?	저 건물은 무엇입니까 ?	chŏ kŏn·mul·ŭn mu·ŏ·shim·ni·ka
Who was the ... ?	…은 누구였음니까 ?	... ŭn nu·gu·yŏ·ssŭm·ni·ka
architect	건축가	kŏn·ch'uk·ka
artist	예술가	ye·sul·ga
painter	화가	hwa·ga
sculptor	조각가	cho·gak·ka
Who built it ?	누가 그것을 지었나요 ?	nu·ga kŭ·gŏ·sŭl chi·ŏt·na·yo
Who painted that picture ?	저 그림은 누가 그렸읍니까 ?	chŏ kŭ·rim·ŭn nu·ga kŭ·ryŏ · ssŭm · ni · ka
When did he live ?	어느 시대 사람입니까 ?	ŏ·nŭ shi·dae sa·ram·im·ni·ka
When was it built ?	그것은 언제 건립되었나요 ?	kŭ·gŏ·sŭn ŏn·je kŏl·lip·toe·ŏn·na·yo
Where's the house where ... lived ?	…이 살던 집은 어디입니까 ?	... i sal·dŏn chi·bŭn ŏ·di·im·ni·ka
We're interested in ...	…에 흥미를 갖고 있읍니다.	... e hŭng·mi·rŭl kat·ko i·ssŭm·ni·da
antiques	골동품	kol·tong·p'um
archaeology	고고학	ko·go·hak
art	예술	ye·sul
botany	식물학	shik·mul·hak
ceramics	도자기	to·ja·gi
coins	옛날 주화	yet·nal chu·hwa
fine arts	미술	mi·sul
furniture	가구	ka·gu
geology	지질학	chi·jil·hak
history	역사	yŏk·sa
medicine	의학	ŭi·hak
music	음악	ŭm·ak
natural history	박물학	pang·mul·hak
ornithology	조류학	cho·ryu·hak
painting	회화	hoe·hwa
pottery	도예	to·ye
sculpture	조각	cho·gak
wildlife	야생 생물	ya·saeng saeng·mul
zoology	동물학	tong·mul·hak
Where's the ... department ?	…부는 어딥니까 ?	... pu·nŭn ŏ·dim·ni·ka

Just the adjective you've been looking for . . .

It's . . .	. . .군요.	. . . gun·yo
amazing	놀랍	nol·lap
awful	지독하	chi·dok·ha
beautiful	아름답	a·rŭm·dap
gloomy	음침하	ŭm·ch'im·ha
hideous	무시무시하	mu·shi·mu·shi·ha
interesting	재미있	chae·mi·it
magnificent	으리으리하	ŭ·ri·ŭ·ri·ha
monumental	당당하	tang·dang·ha
overwhelming	압도적이	ap·to·jŏ·gi
sinister	불길하	pul·gil·ha
strange	기묘하	ki·myŏ·ha
stupendous	거대하	kŏ·dae·ha
superb	훌륭하	hul·lyung·ha
terrible	지독하	chi·dok·ha
terrifying	무섭	mu·sŏp
tremendous	어마어마하	ŏ·ma·ŏ·ma·ha
ugly	보기 흉하	po·gi hyung·ha

Church services

Korea has about 10 million Christians, approximately 25% of the total population. Churches of many denominations abound in every city.

Is there a . . . near here?	이 근처에 …이 있읍니까?	i kŭn·ch'ŏ·e . . . i i·ssŭm·ni·ka
Orthodox church	그리스 정교회	kŭ·ri·sŭ chŏng·gyo·hoe
Protestant church	프로테스탄트 교회	p'ŭ·ro·t'ĕ·sŭ·t'an·t'ŭ kyo·hoe
Catholic church	가톨릭 성당	ka·t'ol·lik sŏng·dang
synagogue	유대교 회당	yu·dae·gyo hoe·dang
mosque	회교사원	hoe·gyo·sa·wŏn
At what time is mass/ the service?	미사/예배는 몇시에 있읍니까?	mi·sa/ye·bae·nŭn myŏt·shi·e i·ssŭm·ni·ka
Where can I find a priest/minister who speaks English?	영어를 할 줄 아는 신부님/목사님은 어디 가면 만날 수 있읍니까?	yŏng·ŏ·rŭl hal jul a·nŭn shin·bu·nim/mok·sa·nim·ŭn ŏ·di ka·myŏn man·nal su i·ssŭm·ni·ka

Relaxing

Cinema (movies)—Theatre

The cinema programme normally consists of one feature film (occasionally two), a short documentary or a newsreel and advertisements. City centre cinemas get very busy so it's worth buying a ticket in advance to avoid disappointment.

Theatre openings depend entirely on drama groups. You can find out what's playing from local English-language newspapers. At major Western-style hotels you'll easily find publications of the type "This Week in ...". Foreign films aren't dubbed but run in their original version, subtitled in Korean.

Have you a copy of "This Week in Seoul"?	"이 주일의 서울"이 있읍 니까?	i·ju·il·ŭi sŏ·ul·i i·ssŭm·ni·ka
What's on at the cinema tonight?	오늘밤 영화관에서는 무 엇을 상영하고 있나요?	o·nŭl·bam yŏng·hwa·gwan·e· sŏ·nŭn mu·ŏ·sŭl sang·yŏng·ha· go in·na·yo
What's playing at the National Theatre?	국립 극장에서는 무엇을 상연하고 있나요?	kung·nip kŭk·jang·e·sŏ·nŭn mu·ŏ·sŭl sang·yŏn·ha·go in·na·yo
What sort of play is it?	그것은 어떤 연극입니 까?	kŭ·gŏ·sŭn ŏ·ttŏn yŏn·gŭk· im·ni·ka
Who's it by?	원작자는 누구입니까?	wŏn·jak·cha·nŭn nu·gu·im·ni·ka
Can you recommend (a) ...?	…을 가르쳐 주시겠어 요?	... ŭl ka·rŭ·ch'yŏ chu· shi·ge·ssŏ·yo
good film	좋은 영화	cho·ŭn yŏng·hwa
comedy	희극	hŭi·gŭk
drama	드라마	dŭ·ra·ma
musical	음악극	ŭm·ak·kŭk
revue	시사 풍자극	shi·sa p'ung·ja·gŭk
something light	뭔가 가벼운 것	mwŏn·ga ka·byŏ·un kŏt

thriller	스릴 영화	sŭ·ril yŏng·hwa
Western	서부극	sŏ·bu·gŭk
At what theatre is that new play by ... showing?	…의 신작극은 어디서 상연되고 있읍니까?	... ŭi shin·jak·kŭk·ŭn ŏ·di·sŏ sang·yŏn·doe·go i·ssŭm·ni·ka
Where's that new film by ... playing?	…의 신작 영화는 어디서 상영되고 있읍니까?	... ŭi shin·jak yŏng·hwa·nŭn ŏ·di·sŏ sang·yŏng·doe·go i·ssŭm·ni·ka
Who's in it?	누가 출연합니까?	nu·ga ch'ul·yŏn·ham·ni·ka
Who's playing the lead?	주연은 누구입니까?	chu·yŏn·ŭn nu·gu·im·ni·ka
Who's the director?	감독은 누구입니까?	kam·dok·ŭn nu·gu·im·ni·ka
What time does it begin?	그것은 몇시에 시작합니까?	kŭ·gŏ·sŭn myŏt·shi·e shi·jak·ham·ni·ka
What time does the show end?	그 쇼는 몇시에 끝납니까?	kŭ syo·nŭn myŏt·shi·e kŭn·nam·ni·ka
Are there any tickets for tonight?	오늘밤 표가 남아 있읍니까?	o·nŭl·bam p'yo·ga nam·a i·ssŭm·ni·ka
I want to reserve two tickets for the show on Friday evening.	금요일날 저녁 쇼의 표를 두 장 예약하고자 하는데요.	kŭm·yo·il·nal chŏ·nyŏk·sho·ŭi p'yo·rŭl tu·jang ye·yak·ha·go·ja ha·nŭn·de·yo
Can I have a ticket for the matinee on Tuesday?	화요일날 낮 공연의 표를 한 장 구입할 수 있읍니까?	hwa·yo·il·nal nat·kong·yŏn·ŭi p'yo·rŭl han·jang ku·ip·hal·su i·ssŭm·ni·ka
I want a seat in the stalls (orchestra).	1층 맨 앞줄 자리를 원합니다.	il·ch'ŭng maen ap·chul cha·ri·rŭl wŏn·ham·ni·da
Not too far forward/back.	너무 앞자리/뒷자리 말고요.	nŏ·mu ap·cha·ri/twit·cha·ri mal·go·yo
Somewhere in the middle.	가운데쯤.	ka·un·de·chŭm
How much are the seats in the circle (balcony)?	2층석은 얼마입니까?	i·ch'ŭng·sŏk·ŭn ŏl·ma·im·ni·ka
May I have a programme, please?	프로그램을 주시겠어요?	p'ŭ·ro·gŭ·raem·ŭl chu·shi·ge·ssŏ·yo
Can I check this coat?	이 코트를 맡길 수 있읍니까?	i k'o·t'ŭ·rŭl ma·kil·su i·ssŭm·ni·ka
Here's my ticket.	이것이 내 표입니다.	i·gŏ·shi nae p'yo·im·ni·da

A few words on traditional folk theatre and dance

The two major forms of folk dance and theatre unique to Korea are *Nong-ak* and *T'alch'um* or *Kamyŏn-kŭk*.

Nong-ak, or "Farmers' Festival Music and Dance," is the oldest of Korean folk performing arts, dating all the way back to the prehistoric Tribal States period when it was used for ritualistic purposes. The musical instruments are largely from the percussion family and are played by the dancers themselves who wear hats onto which a long paper streamer is tied. As they dance, they twirl the streamers around in a circular fashion.

T'alch'um or **Kamyŏn-kŭk** ("Mask Dance-Drama") represents one of the major forms of traditional folk theatre in Korea today. It was performed continuously on up through the mid-Yi Dynasty period (c. 17th century) as part of both a rite of exorcism and an entertainment form, until the mask players were banished from the royal court in Seoul by the Neo-Confucianists. Thereafter, this dance-drama was dispersed to various regions of the countryside where it evolved into a comic satire that depicted the depravity of the aristocratic ruling classes, the Buddhist clergy, and the triangular relationship of husband, wife, and concubine prevalent in the society at the time.

Opera—Ballet—Concert

Where's the opera house ?	오페라 극장은 어디입니까 ?	o·p'e·ra kŭk·chang·ŭn ŏ·di·im·ni·ka
Where's the concert hall ?	음악회장은 어디입니까 ?	ŭm·ak·hoe·jang·ŭn ŏ·di·im·ni·ka
What's on at the opera tonight ?	오늘밤에는 무슨 오페라가 있읍니까 ?	o·nŭl·bam·e·nŭn mu·sŭn o·p'e·ra·ga i·ssŭm·ni·ka
Who's performing ?	누가 출연합니까 ?	nu·ga ch'ul·yŏn·ham·ni·ka

What time does the programme start ?	그 프로는 몇시에 시작합니까?	kǔ p'ǔ·ro·nǔn myǒt·shi·e shi·jak·ham·ni·ka
Which orchestra is playing ?	어느 오케스트라가 연주합니까?	ǒ·nǔ o·k'e·sǔ·t'ǔ·ra·ga yǒn·ju·ham·ni·ka
What are they playing ?	무엇을 연주합니까?	mu·ǒ·sǔl yǒn·ju·ham·ni·ka
Who's the conductor ?	지휘자는 누구입니까?	chi·hwi·ja·nǔn nu·gu·im·ni·ka

---

Possible answers

미안합니다. 매진되었읍니다.	I'm sorry. We're sold out.
1층 앞자리는 조금밖에 남아 있지 않습니다.	There are only a few seats in the circle (balcony) left.
표 좀 보여주시겠어요?	May I see your ticket ?

Nightclubs

Nightclubs are pretty much the same the world over, particularly when it comes to inflated prices. You can expect to pay a cover charge. Your drinks will be expensive. The girls sitting around aren't there because they like the decor.

There are some reasonably-priced places that provide good entertainment, so ask around. But find out the prices before you order and allow for the various surcharges.

For most nightclubs a dark suit is sufficient.

Can you recommend a good nightclub ?	좋은 나이트 클럽을 소개해주시겠읍니까?	cho·ǔn na·i·t'ǔ k'ǔl·lǒb·ǔl so·gae·hae chu·shi·ge·ssǔm·ni·ka
Is there a floor show ?	플로어 쇼가 있읍니까?	p'ǔl·lo·ǒ syo·ga i·ssǔm·ni·ka
What time does the floor show start ?	플로어 쇼는 몇시에 시작합니까?	p'ǔl·lo·ǒ syo·nǔn myǒt·shi·e shi·jak·ham·ni·ka
Is evening dress necessary ?	야회복을 입을 필요가 있읍니까?	ya·hoe·bo·gǔl i·bǔl p'i·ryo·ga i·ssǔm·ni·ka

RELAXING

And once inside . . .

A table for two, please.	2인용 테이블을 부탁합니다.	i·in·yong t'e·i·bǔ·rǔl pu·t'ak·ham·ni·da
My name is ... I've reserved a table for four.	나는 …입니다. 4인용 테이블을 예약했읍니다.	na·nǔn ... im·ni·da sa·in·yong t'e·i·bǔ·rǔl ye·yak·hae·ssǔm·ni·da
We don't have a reservation.	예약하지 않았읍니다.	ye·yak·ha·ji a·na·ssǔm·ni·da

Note: The standard closing time for drinking places in Korea is midnight, although a fair number of coffee shops, roadside carts and restaurants stay open all night. If you like, you can also spend the night in a cinema in Seoul: some show films all through the night during weekends.

Kisaeng

Kisaeng are hostess-entertainers now only found at a very few top-class traditional Korean restaurants. At one time in Korean history, these women were trained from childhood in the arts of calligraphy, poetry, music, singing, dancing, and archery. They were regarded as highly accomplished individuals, companions of aristocrats, ranking government officials, the literati, and, in a later period, wealthy business magnates. They rarely married and, more often than not, became the concubines of their affluent clientele. Though this is no longer the case in modern Korea, the *kisaeng* of today, nevertheless, still remain charming and beautiful companions with whom whiling away a few hours at a restaurant can make an evening's entertainment all the difference in the world. Of course, the visitor should keep in mind that generous tipping is the order of the day.

Dancing

Where can we go dancing ?	어디서 춤을 출 수 있읍니까?	ŏ·di·sŏ ch'um·ŭl ch'ul·su i·ssŭm·ni·ka
Is there a dance hall anywhere here ?	이 근방에 댄스홀이 있읍니까?	i kŭn·bang·e taen·sŭ·hol·i i·ssŭm·ni·ka
There's a dance at the ...	...에 무도회가 있읍니다.	... e mu·do·hoe·ga i·ssŭm·ni·da
Would you like to dance ?	춤추러 갈까요?	ch'um·ch'u·rŏ kal·ka·yo
May I have this dance ?	함께 추실까요?	ham·ke ch'u·shil·ka·yo

Do you happen to play ... ?

On rainy days, this page may solve your problems.

Do you happen to play chess ?	서양 장기를 두시나요?	sŏ·yang chang·gi·rŭl tu·shi·na·yo
I'm afraid I don't.	두지 않습니다.	tu·ji an·sŭm·ni·da
No. But I'll give you a game of draughts (checkers).	아뇨. 하지만 체커라면 상대해드리지요.	a·nyo. ha·ji·man ch'e·k'ŏ·ra·myŏn sang·dae·hae tŭ·ri·ji·yo
king	킹	k'ing
queen	퀸	k'win
castle (rook)	룩	ruk
bishop	비숍	pi·syop
knight	나이트	na·i·t'ŭ
pawn	폰	p'on
Do you play cards ?	트럼프를 하십니까?	t'ŭ·rŏm·p'ŭ·rŭl ha·shim·ni·ka
bridge	브리지	pŭ·ri·ji
whist	휘스트	hwi·sŭ·t'ŭ
pontoon (blackjack)	블랙잭	pŭl·laek·chaek
poker	포커	p'o·k'ŏ
ace	에이스	e·i·sŭ
king	킹	k'ing
queen	퀸	k'win
jack	잭	chaek
joker	조커	cho·k'ŏ

RELAXING

Sport

In addition to the traditional martial art of *t'aekwŏndo,* practically every sport played in the West with the exception of American football and rugby, is also popular in Korea (golf, tennis, soccer, basketball, skiing, swimming, table tennis, etc.). Baseball, introduced into Korea in 1906, has gained such wide popularity and enthusiasm that there is now a pro-baseball league. Boxing and wrestling have also gained wide popularity, while Korean traditional-style wrestling, called *ssirŭm,* can still be seen at various tournaments held both in the capital city of Seoul and in provincial cities. These are exciting as well as interesting events, accompanied by time-honoured ceremony and traditional folk music and dance.

Where's the nearest golf course ?	가장 가까운 골프장은 어 딥니까?	ka·jang ka·ka·un kol·p'ŭ·jang·ŭn ŏ·dim·ni·ka
Where are the tennis courts ?	테니스장은 어딥니까?	t'e·ni·sŭ·jang·ŭn ŏ·dim·ni·ka
Can I/we hire ...?	…을 빌릴 수 있읍니까?	... ŭl pil·lil·su i·ssŭm·ni·ka
golf clubs	골프 채	kol·p'ŭ ch'ae
equipment	도구	to·gu
rackets	라켓	ra·k'et
What's the charge per hour/day/round ?	한 시간/하루/1 라운드에 요금이 얼맙니까?	han shi·gan/ha·ru/il·la·un·dŭ·e yo·gŭm·i ŏl·mam·ni·ka
What's the admission charge ?	입장료는 얼맙니까?	ip·chang·ryo·nŭn ŏl·mam·ni·ka
Is there a swimming pool here ?	여기에 수영장이 있읍니까?	yŏ·gi·e su·yŏng·jang·i i·ssŭm·ni·ka
Is it open-air or indoor ?	옥외입니까, 실내입니까?	ok·oe·im·ni·ka shil·nae·im·ni·ka
Is it heated ?	난방이 되어 있읍니까?	nan·bang·i toe·ŏ i·ssŭm·ni·ka
Is there any good fishing around here ?	이 근처에 좋은 낚시터가 있읍니까?	i kŭn·ch'ŏ·e cho·ŭn nak·shi·t'ŏ·ga i·ssŭm·ni·ka
Is there any *ssirŭm* match this evening ?	오늘 저녁에 씨름 경기가 있읍니까?	o·nŭl chŏ·nyŏ·ge ssi·rŭm kyŏng·gi·ga i·ssŭm·ni·ka

On the beach

What's the beach like?	어떤 해수욕장입니까?	ŏ·tŏn hae·su·yok·chang·im·ni·ka
sand/shingle/rocky	모래밭/자갈밭/갯바위	mo·rae·bat/cha·gal·bat/kaet·pa·wi
Is it safe for swimming?	수영해도 안전합니까?	su·yŏng·hae·do an·jŏn·ham·ni·ka
Is there a lifeguard?	인명구조원이 있읍니까?	in·myŏng·gu·jo·wŏn·i i·ssŭm·ni·ka
Is it safe for children?	아이들에게도 안전합니까?	a·i·dŭl·e·ge·do an·jŏn·ham·ni·ka
It's very calm.	매우 잔잔합니다.	mae·u chan·jan·ham·ni·da
There are some big waves.	더러 큰 파도가 칩니다.	tŏ·rŏ k'ŭn p'a·do·ga ch'im·ni·da
Are there any dangerous currents?	위험한 조류가 있읍니까?	wi·hŏm·han cho·ryu·ga i·ssŭm·ni·ka
What time is high tide?	만조 시각은 몇시입니까?	man·jo shi·gak·ŭn myŏt·shi·im·ni·ka
What time is low tide?	간조 시각은 몇시입니까?	kan·jo shi·gak·ŭn myŏt·shi·im·ni·ka
What's the temperature of the water?	수온은 몇도입니까?	su·on·ŭn myŏt·to·im·ni·ka
I want to hire ...	…을 빌리고 싶은데요.	... ŭl pil·li·go shi·p'ŭn·de·yo
an air mattress	에어 매트리스	e·ŏ mae·t'ŭ·ri·sŭ
a bathing hut	탈의장	t'al·ŭi·jang
a deck chair	갑판용 의자	kap·p'an·yong ŭi·ja
skin-diving equipment	스킨다이빙용 장비	sŭ·k'in·da·i·bing·yong chang·bi
a sunshade	해가리개	hae·ga·ri·gae
a surfboard	파도타기용 널빤지	p'a·do·t'a·gi·yong nŏl·pan·ji
a tent	텐트	t'en·t'ŭ
some waterskis	수상 스키	su·sang sŭ·k'i
Where can I rent ...?	…은 어디서 빌릴 수 있읍니까?	... ŭn ŏ·di·sŏ pil·lil·su i·ssŭm·ni·ka
a canoe	카누	k'a·nu
a rowboat	노젓는 보트	no·jŏt·nŭn bo·t'ŭ
a motorboat	모터보트	mo·t'ŏ·bo·t'ŭ
a sailboat	요트	yo·t'ŭ

| What's the charge per hour ? | 시간당 요금은 얼마입니까? | shi·gan·dang yo·gŭm·ŭn ŏl·ma·im·ni·ka |

사 유 지
PRIVATE BEACH

수 영 금 지
NO BATHING

Obviously, not the place for us. Let's move on.

Winter sports

I'd like to go to a skating rink.	스케이트장에 가고 싶은데요.	sŭ·k'e·i·t'ŭ·jang·e ka·go shi·p'ŭn·de·yo
Is there one near here ?	요 근처에 있읍니까?	yo kŭn·ch'ŏ·e i·ssŭm·ni·ka
I want to rent some skates.	스케이트를 빌리고 싶은데요.	sŭ·k'e·i·t'ŭ·rŭl pil·li·go shi·p'ŭn·de·yo
What are the skiing conditions like at ... ?	...에서의 스키 조건은 어떻습니까?	... e·sŏ·ŭi sŭ·k'i cho·gŏn·ŭn ŏ·tŏt·sŭm·ni·ka
The snow is a little soft.	눈이 좀 부드럽습니다.	nun·i chom pu·dŭ·rŏp·sŭm·ni·da
Can I take skiing lessons there ?	거기서 스키 교습을 받을 수 있읍니까?	kŏ·gi·sŏ sŭ·k'i kyo·sŭp·ŭl pa·dŭl·su i·ssŭm·ni·ka
Is there a ski lift ?	스키 리프트가 있읍니까?	sŭ·k'i ri·p'ŭ·t'ŭ·ga i·ssŭm·ni·ka
I want to rent some skiing equipment.	스키 용구를 빌리고 싶은데요.	sŭ·k'i yong·gu·rŭl pil·li·go shi·p'ŭn·de·yo

RELAXING

Countryside—Camping

If you want to explore the Korean countryside, here is a few
phrases and a list of words that may be useful to you.

How far is it to ...?	…까지 얼마나 됩니까?	... ka·ji ŏl·ma·na toem·ni·ka
How far is the next village?	다음 마을까지 얼마나 됩니까?	ta·ŭm ma·ŭl·ka·ji ŏl·ma·na toem·ni·ka
Are we on the right road to ...?	이것이 …으로 가는 길이 맞습니까?	i·gŏ·shi ... ŭ·ro ka·nŭn ki·ri mat·sŭm·ni·ka
Where does this road lead to?	이 길은 어디로 가는 길 입니까?	i ki·rŭn ŏ·di·ro ka·nŭn ki·rim·ni·ka
Can you show us on the map where we are?	이 지도에서 우리가 있는 곳을 가리킬 수 있읍니까?	i chi·do·e·sŏ u·ri·ga in·nŭn ko·sŭl ka·ri·k'il·su i·ssŭm·ni·ka

Landmarks

barn	헛간	hŏt·kan
bridge	다리	ta·ri
brook	개울	kae·ul
building	건물	kŏn·mul
canal	운하	un·ha
cliff	벼랑	pyŏ·rang
copse	덤불	tŏm·bul
cornfield	밀밭	mil·bat
cottage	오두막	o·du·mak
farm	농가	nong·ga
ferry	나룻배	na·rut·pae
field	들	tŭl
footpath	오솔길	o·sol·gil
forest	숲	sup
hamlet	작은 마을	cha·gŭn ma·ŭl
heath	관목	kwan·mok
hill	언덕	ŏn·dŏk
house	집	chip
inn	여인숙	yŏ·in·suk

CAMPING

CAMPING

lake	호수	ho·su
marsh	소택지	so·t'aek·chi
moorland	황야	hwang·ya
mountain	산	san
mountain range	산맥	san·maek
path	오솔길	o·sol·gil
peak	산꼭대기	san·kok·tae·gi
plantation	농원	nong·wŏn
pond	연못	yŏn·mot
pool	풀	p'ul
river	강	kang
road	길	kil
sea	바다	pa·da
spring	샘	saem
stream	시내	shi·nae
swamp	습지	sŭp·chi
track	소로	so·ro
tree	나무	na·mu
valley	골짜기	kol·cha·gi
village	마을	ma·ŭl
vineyard	포도원	p'o·do·wŏn
water	물	mul
waterfall	폭포	p'ok·p'o
well	우물	u·mŭl
wood	숲	sup

What's the name of the river?	이 강의 이름이 뭡니까?	i kang·ŭi i·rŭm·i mwŏm·ni·ka
How high is that mountain?	저 산의 높이는 얼마나 됩니까?	chŏ san·ŭi no·p'i·nŭn ŏl·ma·na toem·ni·ka
How high are those hills?	저 언덕의 높이는 얼마나 됩니까?	chŏ ŏn·dŏk·ŭi no·p'i·nŭn ŏl·ma·na toem·ni·ka
Is there a scenic route to ...?	...으로 가는 경치 좋은 길이 있읍니까?	... ŭro ka·nŭn kyŏng·ch'i cho·ŭn ki·ri i·ssŭm·ni·ka

... and if you're tired of walking, you can always try hitch-hiking, though you may have to wait a long time for a lift.

Can you give me a lift to ...?	...까지 태워다 주시겠어요?	... ka·ji t'ae·wŏ·da chu·shi·ge·ssŏ·yo

Camping

There are a fair number of camping sites in Korea. You can also camp on private land, but get permission from the owner first.

Can we camp here?	여기에서 캠프를 해도 됩니까?	yŏ·gi·e·sŏ k'aem·p'ŭ·rŭl hae·do toem·ni·ka
Is this an official camping site?	이곳은 공인 캠프장입니까?	i·go·sŭn kong·in k'aem·p'ŭ·jang·im·ni·ka
Is there drinking water?	먹는 물이 있읍니까?	mŏng·nŭn mu·ri i·ssŭm·ni·ka
Are there ...?	···이 있읍니까?	... i i·ssŭm·ni·ka
baths	욕실	yok·shil
showers	샤워	sya·wŏ
toilets	화장실	hwa·jang·shil
shopping facilities	매점	mae·jŏm
Is there a youth hostel anywhere near here?	이 근처에 유스 호스텔이 있읍니까?	i kŭn·ch'ŏ·e yu·sŭ ho·sŭ·t'el·i i·ssŭm·ni·ka
Do you know anyone who can put us up for the night?	우리를 하룻밤 묵게 해줄 만한 사람을 아십니까?	u·ri·rŭl ha·rut·pam muk·ke hae·jul·man·han sa·ram·ŭl a·shim·ni·ka

In tourist resort areas in Korea, one can usually find both *yŏgwans* (inns) and youth hostels. The inns are mostly Korean-style where the guest is provided with a mattress, blanket, and pillow, and sleeps on the heated floor (*ondol*).

A chain of youth hostels has been established in many of the provinces, and such facilities are open to international members. Membership is open at any of their branches.

Making friends

Introduction

Here are a few phrases to get you started.

How are you?	안녕하십니까?	an·nyŏng·ha·shim·ni·ka
Very well, thank you.	네, 덕분에.	ne, tŏk·pun·e
How's it going?	어떠십니까?	ŏ·tŏ·shim·ni·ka
Fine, thanks. And you?	잘 지냅니다, 덕분에. 어 떠신지요?	chal chi·naem·ni·da tŏk· pun·e ŏ·tŏ·shin·ji·yo
May I introduce Miss Philips?	필립양을 소개할까요?	p'il·lip·yang·ŭl so·gae·hal· ka·yo
I'd like you to meet a friend of mine.	내 친구를 소개하겠습니 다.	nae ch'in·gu·rŭl so·gae· ha·ge·ssŭm·ni·da
John, this is ...	존, 이 분은 …이에요.	chyon, i·bun·ŭn ... i·e·yo
My name's ...	저는 …이라고 합니다.	chŏ·nŭn ... i·ra·go ham· ni·da
Nice to meet you.	만나뵈어 반갑습니다.	man·na·boe·ŏ pan·gap·sŭm· ni·da

Follow-up

How long have you been here?	여기 오신 지 얼마나 되 었읍니까?	yŏ·gi o·shin·ji ŏl·ma·na toe·ŏ·ssŭm·ni·ka
We've been here a week.	1주일 됩니다.	il·chu·il toem·ni·da
Is this your first visit?	여기는 처음 오십니까?	yŏ·gi·nŭn ch'ŏ·ŭm o·shim· ni·ka
No, we came here last year.	아뇨, 작년에 왔읍니다.	a·nyo, chang·gyŏn·e wa· ssŭm·ni·da
Are you enjoying your stay?	여기가 마음에 드십니 까?	yŏ·gi·ga ma·ŭ·me tŭ·shim·ni· ka

Yes, I like ... very much.	네, …은 아주 마음에 듭니다.	ne ...ŭn a·ju ma·ŭm·e tŭm·ni·da
Are you on your own?	혼자십니까?	hon·ja·shim·ni·ka
I'm with ...	…와 함께 있읍니다.	... wa ham·ke i·ssŭm·ni·da
my husband	남편	nam·p'yŏn
my wife	아내	a·nae
my family	가족	ka·jok
my parents	부모님	pu·mo·nim
some friends	친구들	ch'in·gu·dŭl
Where do you come from?	어디서 오셨읍니까?	ŏ·di·sŏ o·syŏ·ssŭm·ni·ka
What part of ... do you come from?	…의 어느 고장에서 오셨읍니까?	...ŭi ŏ·nŭ ko·jang·e·sŏ o·syŏ·ssŭm·ni·ka
I'm from ...	나는 …에서 왔읍니다.	na·nŭn ...e·sŏ wa·ssŭm·ni·da
Do you live here?	여기 사십니까?	yŏ·gi sa·shim·ni·ka
I'm a student.	나는 학생입니다.	na·nŭn hak·saeng·im·ni·da
What are you studying?	무엇을 공부하시는지요?	mu·ŏ·sŭl kong·bu·ha·shi·nŭn·ji·yo
We're here on holiday.	휴가로 왔읍니다.	hyu·ga·ro wa·ssŭm·ni·da
I'm here on a business trip.	볼일이 있어서 왔읍니다.	pol·i·ri i·ssŏ·sŏ wa·ssŭm·ni·da
What business are you in?	무슨 일을 하시는지요?	mu·sŭn i·rŭl ha·shi·nŭn·ji·yo
I hope we'll see you again soon.	또 뵙게 되기를 바랍니다.	to poep·ke toe·gi·rŭl pa·ram·ni·da
See you later/See you tomorrow.	그럼 또 뵙겠읍니다/내일 또 뵙겠읍니다.	kŭ·rŏm to poep·ke·ssŭm·ni·da/nae·il to poep·ke·ssŭm·ni·da
I'm sure we'll run into each other again.	또 만나뵙게 되겠지요.	to man·na·poep·ke toe·get·chi·yo

The weather

They talk about the weather just as much in Korea as they do in Britain So ...

What a lovely day !	참 좋은 날씨군요 !	ch'am cho·ŭn nal·ssi·gun·yo
What awful weather.	날씨 참 고약하군요.	nal·ssi ch'am ko·yak·ha·gun·yo
Isn't it cold today ?	오늘은 춥지요 ?	o·nŭ·rŭn ch'up·chi·yo
Isn't it hot today ?	오늘은 덥지요 ?	o·nŭ·rŭn tŏp·chi·yo
Is it usually as warm as this ?	늘 이렇게 따뜻합니까 ?	nŭl i·rŏk'e ta·tŭt·ham·ni·ka
It's very foggy, isn't it ?	심한 안개군요.	shim·han an·gae·gun·yo
What's the temperature outside ?	바깥 기온은 얼마나 됩니까 ?	pa·kat ki·on·ŭn ŏl·ma·na toem·ni·ka
The wind is very strong.	바람이 세게 붑니다.	pa·ram·i se·ge pum·ni·da

Invitations

My wife and I would like you to dine with us on ...	⋯에 아내와 함께 당신을 저녁 식사에 초대하고 싶은데요.	... e a·nae·wa ham·ke tang·shin·ŭl chŏ·nyŏk shik·sa·e ch'o·dae·ha·go shi·pŭn·de·yo
Can you come to dinner tomorrow night ?	내일밤 만찬에 와 주시겠읍니까 ?	nae·il·bam man·ch'an·e wa·ju·shi·ge·ssŭm·ni·ka
We're giving a small party tomorrow night. I do hope you can come.	내일밤에 조촐한 파티를 열려고 합니다. 와주셨으면 하는데요.	nae·il·bam·e cho·ch'ol·han p'a·t'i·rŭl yŏl·lyŏ·go ham·ni·da wa·ju·syŏ·ssŭ·myŏn ha·nŭn·de·yo
Can you come round for cocktails this evening ?	오늘밤 칵테일 파티에 와 주시겠읍니까 ?	o·nŭl·bam k'ak·t'e·il p'a·t'i·e wa·ju·shi·ge·ssŭm·ni·ka
There's a party. Are you coming ?	파티가 있읍니다. 오시겠읍니까 ?	p'a·t'i·ga i·ssŭm·ni·da o·shi·ge·ssŭm·ni·ka

That's very kind of you.	정말 감사합니다.	chŏng·mal kam·sa· ham·ni· da
Great. I'd love to come.	멋지군요. 기꺼이 오겠읍니다.	mŏt·chi·gun·yo ki·kŏ·i o·ge·ssŭm·ni·da
What time shall we come?	몇시에 올까요?	myŏt·shi·e ol·ka·yo
May I bring a friend?	친구를 한 사람 데리고 와도 됩니까?	ch'in·gu·rŭl han·sa·ram te·ri·go wa·do toem·ni·ka
I'm afraid we've got to go now.	이제 가봐야 되겠는데요.	i·je ka·bwa·ya toe·gen· nŭn·de·yo
Next time you must come and visit us.	다음번에는 우리집에도 오셔야 합니다.	ta·ŭm·bŏn·e·nŭn u·ri·jip·e·do o·syŏ·ya ham·ni·da
Thank you very much for an enjoyable evening.	덕택에 즐거운 저녁을 보 냈읍니다.	tŏk·t'ae·ge chŭl·gŏ·un chŏ· nyŏ·gŭl po·nae·ssŭm·ni·da
Thanks for the party. It was great.	파티에 초대해 주셔서 감 사합니다. 정말 훌륭했읍 니다.	p'a·t'i·e ch'o·dae·hae chu· syŏ·sŏ kam·sa·ham·ni·da chŏng·mal hul·lyung·hae· ssŭm·ni·da

Dating

Do you mind if I smoke?	담배 피워도 될까요?	tam·bae p'i·wŏ·do toel·ka·yo
Would you like a cigarette?	담배 피우시겠읍니까?	tam·bae p'i·u·shi·ge·ssŭm· ni·ka
Have you got a light, please?	불 좀 빌릴까요?	pul·jom pil·lil·ka·yo?
Can I get you a drink?	한 잔 하시겠읍니까?	han·jan ha·shi·ge·ssŭm·ni· ka?
Excuse me, could you help me, please?	죄송하지만, 좀 도와 주 시겠어요?	choe·song·ha·ji·man chom to·wa chu·shi·ge·ssŏ·yo
I'm lost. Can you show me the way to ...?	길을 잃었는데요, …으로 가는 길을 가리켜 주시겠 어요?	ki·rŭl i·rŏn·nŭn·de·yo ... ŭ·ro ka·nŭn ki·rŭl ka·ri·k'yŏ chu· shi·ge·ssŏ·yo
Are you waiting for someone?	누구를 기다리고 계십니 까?	nu·gu·rŭl ki·da·ri·go kye· shim·ni·ka?

Are you free this evening ?	오늘 저녁 시간이 있읍니까 ?	o·nŭl chŏ·nyŏk shi·gan·i i·ssŭm·ni·ka?
Would you like to go out with me tonight ?	오늘밤 나와 함께 외출하시지 않겠읍니까 ?	o·nŭl·bam na·wa ham·ke oe·ch'ul·ha·shi·ji an·k'e·ssŭm·ni·ka
Would you like to go dancing ?	춤추러 가지 않겠읍니까 ?	ch'um·ch'u·rŏ ka·ji an·k'e·ssŭm·ni·ka
I know a good dance hall.	좋은 댄스 홀을 알고 있읍니다.	cho·ŭn daen·sŭ ho·rŭl al·go i·ssŭm·ni·da
Shall we go to the cinema (movies)?	영화구경 가실까요 ?	yŏng·hwa·ku·gyŏng ka·shil·ka·yo
Would you like to go for a drive ?	드라이브나 할까요 ?	dŭ·ra·i·bŭ·na hal·ka·yo
I'd love to, thank you.	좋습니다, 고마와요.	cho·ssŭm·ni·da ko·ma·wa·yo
Where shall we meet ?	어디서 만날까요 ?	ŏ·di·sŏ man·nal·ka·yo
I'll pick you up at your hotel.	호텔로 모시러 갈께요.	ho·t'el·lo mo·shi·rŏ kal·ke·yo
I'll call for you at 8.	8시에 모시러 갈께요.	yŏ·dŏl·shi·e mo·shi·rŏ kal·ke·yo
May I take you home ?	댁까지 태워다 드릴까요 ?	taek·ka·ji t'ae·wŏ·da tŭ·ril·ka·yo
Can I see you again tomorrow ?	내일 또 뵐 수 있을까요 ?	nae·il to poel·su i·ssŭl·ka·yo
Thank you, it's been a wonderful evening.	고맙습니다. 아주 즐거운 저녁이었어요.	ko·map·sŭm·ni·da a·ju chŭl·gŏ·un chŏ·nyŏk·i·ŏ·ssŏ·yo
What's your telephone number ?	전화번호는 몇번입니까 ?	chŏn·hwa·bŏn·ho·nŭn myŏt·pŏn·im·ni·ka?
Do you live alone ?	혼자 사십니까 ?	hon·ja sa·shim·ni·ka?

Shopping guide

This shopping guide is designed to help you find what you want with ease, accuracy and speed. It features:

1. a list of all major shops, stores and services;

2. some general expressions required when shopping to allow you to be specific and selective;

3. full details of the shops and services most likely to concern you. Here you will find advice, alphabetical lists of items and conversion charts listed under the headings below.

Shops, stores and services

If you have a pretty clear idea of what you want before you set out, do a little homework first. Look under the appropriate heading, pick out the article and find a suitable description for it (colour, material, etc.).

Shops in Korea usually open between 9 and 10 a.m. and stay open generally up to 9 p.m., except department stores which open at 10.30 a.m. and close at 7.30 p.m. Many shops are open on Saturdays but close on Sundays.

Some stores in the larger towns offer a discount for traveller's checks or arrange sales tax rebates.

Where's the nearest ...?	가장 가까운 …은 어디 있읍니까?	ka·jang ka·ka·un ... ŭn ŏ·di i·ssŭm·ni·ka
antique shop	골동품점	kol·tong·p'um·jŏm
art gallery	화랑	hwa·rang
baker's	빵집	pang·jip
bank	은행	ŭn·haeng
barber's	이발소	i·bal·so
beauty parlour	미장원	mi·jang·wŏn
bookshop	서점	sŏ·jŏm
bookstall	신문 잡지 매점	shin·mun chap·chi mae·jŏm
butcher's	정육점	chŏng·yuk·chŏm
cable office	전신국	chŏn·shin·guk
camera store	카메라점	k'a·me·ra·jŏm
candy store	과자점	kwa·ja·jŏm
chemist's	약국	yak·kuk
cigar store	담배 가게	tam·bae ka·ge
confectionery	과자점	kwa·ja·jŏm
dairy	우유 가게	u·yu ka·ge
delicatessen	식료품점	shing·nyo·p'um·jŏm
dentist	치과	ch'i·kwa
department store	백화점	paek·hwa·jŏm
doctor	의사	ŭi·sa
draper's (dry goods store)	포목상	p'o·mok·sang
dressmaker's	양장점	yang·jang·jŏm
drugstore	약방	yak·pang

dry cleaner's	드라이클리닝집	tŭ·ra·i·k'ŭl·li·ning·jip
filling station	주유소	chu·yu·so
fishmonger	생선 가게	saeng·sŏn ka·ge
florist's	꽃집	kot·jip
furrier	모피상	mo·p'i·sang
garage	차고	ch'a·go
greengrocer's	채소 가게	ch'ae·so ka·ge
grocery	식료품점	shing·nyo·p'um·jŏm
hairdresser's (ladies)	미장원	mi·jang·wŏn
hardware store	철물점	ch'ŏl·mul·chŏm
hat shop	모자 가게	mo·ja ka·ge
hospital	병원	pyŏng·wŏn
jeweller's	보석상	po·sŏk·sang
launderette	셀프 서비스 세탁소	sel·p'ŭ sŏ·bi·sŭ se·t'ak·so
laundry	세탁소	se·t'ak·so
liquor store	술집	sul·chip
market	시장	shi·jang
milliner's	부인 모자점	pu·in mo·ja·jŏm
news agent's	신문 판매점	shin·mun p'an·mae·jŏm
newsstand	신문 매점	shin·mun mae·jŏm
optician	안경점	an·gyŏng·jŏm
pastry shop	과자점	kwa·ja·jŏm
pawnbroker	전당포	chŏn·dang·p'o
pharmacy	약국	yak·kuk
photographer	사진사	sa·jin·sa
photo store	사진관	sa·jin·gwan
police station	파출소	p'a·ch'ul·so
post office	우체국	u·ch'e·guk
shirt maker's	와이샤쓰점	wa·i·sya·ssŭ·jŏm
shoemaker's (repairs)	제화점	che·hwa·jŏm
shoe shop	양화점	yang·hwa·jŏm
souvenir shop	선물 가게	sŏn·mul ka·ge
sporting goods shop	운동구점	un·dong·gu·jŏm
stationer's	문방구점	mun·bang·gu·jŏm
supermarket	수퍼마켓	su·p'ŏ·ma·k'et
tailor's	양복점	yang·bok·chŏm
tobacconist's	담배 가게	tam·bae ka·ge
toy shop	완구점	wan·gu·jŏm
travel agent	여행사	yŏ·haeng·sa
veterinarian	수의사	su·ŭi·sa
watchmaker's	시계점	shi·gye·jŏm
wine merchant's	술집	sul·chip

General expressions

Here are some expressions which will be useful to you when you're out shopping.

Where?

Where's there a good...?	좋은 …은 어디 있읍니까?	cho·ŭn ... ŭn ŏ·di i·ssŭm·ni·ka
Where can I find a ...?	…은 어디 있읍니까?	... ŭn ŏ·di i·ssŭm·ni·ka
Where do they sell ...?	…은 어디서 팝니까?	... ŭn ŏ·di·sŏ p'am·ni·ka
Can you recommend an inexpensive ...?	싼 …을 가르쳐 주시겠어요?	ssan ... ŭl ka·rŭ·ch'yŏ chu·shi·ge·ssŏ·yo
Where's the main shopping centre?	쇼핑 센터는 어디에 있읍니까?	syo·p'ing sen·t'ŏ·nŭn ŏ·di·e i·ssŭm·ni·ka
How far is it from here?	여기서 얼마나 멉니까?	yŏ·gi·sŏ ŏl·ma·na mŏm·ni·ka
How do I get there?	거기에는 어떻게 갑니까?	kŏ·gi·e·nŭn ŏ·tŏ·k'e kam·ni·ka

Service

Can you help me?	부탁합니다.	pu·t'ak·ham·ni·da
I'm just looking around.	구경 좀 합니다.	ku·gyŏng chom ham·ni·da
I want ...	…을 사고 싶은데요.	... ŭl sa·go shi·p'ŭn·de·yo
Can you show me some ...?	…을 좀 보여 주시겠어요?	... ŭl chom po·yŏ chu·shi·ge·ssŏ·yo
Have you any ...?	…이 있읍니까?	... i i·ssŭm·ni·ka

That one

Can you show me ...?	…을 보여 주시겠어요?	... ŭl po·yŏ chu·shi·ge·ssŏ·yo
that/those	저것/저것들	chŏ·gŏt/chŏ·gŏt·tŭl
the one in the window	쇼윈도에 있는 것	syo·win·do·e in·nŭn kŏt
It's over there.	저기 있읍니다.	chŏ·gi i·ssŭm·ni·da

Preference

I'd prefer something of better quality.	더 질이 좋은 것을 원합 니다.	tŏ chi·ri cho·ŭn kŏ·sŭl wŏn· ham·ni·da
Can you show me some more?	좀 더 보여 주시겠어요?	chom tŏ po·yŏ chu·shi·ge· ssŏ·yo
Haven't you any-thing ...?	…한 것은 없읍니까?	... han kŏ·sŭn ŏp·sŭm·ni· ka
cheaper/better	더 싼/더 좋은	tŏ ssan/tŏ cho·ŭn
larger/smaller	더 큰/더 작은	tŏ k'ŭn/tŏ cha·gŭn

Defining the article

I'd like a ...	…을 주세요.	... ŭl chu·se·yo
I want a ... one.	…한 것을 원합니다.	... han kŏ·sŭl wŏn· ham·ni·da
big	큰	k'ŭn
cheap	싼	ssan
dark	색깔이 짙은	saek·ka·ri chi·t'ŭn
good	좋은	cho·ŭn
heavy	무거운	mu·gŏ·un
large	큰	k'ŭn
light (weight)	가벼운	ka·byŏ·un
light (colour)	색깔이 옅은	saek·ka·ri yŏ·t'ŭn
rectangular	장방형의	chang·bang·hyŏng·ŭi
round	둥근	tung·gŭn
small	작은	cha·gŭn
square	네모진	ne·mo·jin
I don't want anything too expensive.	너무 비싼 것은 원치 않 습니다.	nŏ·mu pi·ssan kŏ·sŭn wŏn·ch'i an·sŭm·ni·da

How much?

How much is this?	이것은 얼마입니까?	i·gŏ·sŭn ŏl·ma·im·ni·ka
I don't understand.	모르겠는데요.	mo·rŭ·gen·nŭn·de·yo
Please write it down.	써 주세요.	ssŏ chu·se·yo
I don't want to spend more than 10,000 won.	10,000원 이상은 쓰고 싶 지 않아요.	10,000 wŏn i·sang·ŭn ssŭ· go ship·chi a·na·yo

FOR COLOURS, see page 111

SHOPPING GUIDE

Decision

That's just what I want.	내가 원하는 것이 바로 그것입니다.	nae·ga wŏn·ha·nŭn kŏ·shi pa·ro kŭ·gŏ·shim·ni·da
No, I don't like it.	그건 마음에 안듭니다.	kŭ·gŏn ma·ŭm·e an·dŭm·ni·da
I'll take it.	그것을 주세요.	kŭ·gŏ·sŭl chu·se·yo

Ordering

Can you order it for me?	그것을 주문해 주시겠어요?	kŭ·gŏ·sŭl chu·mun·hae chu·shi·ge·ssŏ·yo
How long will it take?	얼마나 걸립니까?	ŏl·ma·na kŏl·lim·ni·ka

Delivery

I'll take it with me.	내가 가지고 가겠읍니다.	nae·ga ka·ji·go ka·ge·ssŭm·ni·da
Deliver it at the ... Hotel.	…호텔로 배달해 주세요.	... ho·t'el·lo pae·dal·hae chu·se·yo
Please send it to this address.	이 주소로 부쳐 주세요.	i chu·so·ro pu·ch'yŏ chu·se·yo
Will I have any difficulty with the customs?	세관에서 문제되는 일은 없을까요?	se·gwan·e·sŏ mun·je·doe·nŭn i·rŭn ŏp·sŭl·ka·yo

Paying

How much is it?	얼마입니까?	ŏl·ma·im·ni·ka
Can I pay by traveller's cheque?	여행자 수표로 지불해도 됩니까?	yŏ·haeng·ja su·p'yo·ro chi·bul·hae·do toem·ni·ka
Do you accept credit cards?	크레딧카드도 받습니까?	k'ŭ·re·dit·k'a·dŭ·do pa·ssŭm·ni·ka
Haven't you made a mistake in the bill?	계산서에 틀림이 없습니까?	kye·san·sŏ·e t'ŭl·lim·i ŏp·sŭm·ni·ka
Can I have a receipt, please?	영수증을 받을 수 있어요?	yŏng·su·jŭng·ŭl pa·dŭl·su i·ssŏ·yo
Will you wrap it, please?	포장해 주겠어요?	p'o·jang·hae chu·ge·ssŏ·yo
Do you have a carrier bag?	쇼핑 백이 있읍니까?	syo·p'ing·bae·gi i·ssŭm·ni·ka

Anything else?

No, thanks, that's all.	이것으로 됐읍니다.	i·gŏ·sŭ·ro twe·ssŭm·ni·da
Yes, I want . . . / Show me . . .	네, …을 원합니다. / …을 보여 주세요.	ne . . . ŭl wŏn·ham·ni·da/ . . . ŭl po·yŏ chu·se·yo
Thank you. Goodbye.	고맙습니다. 안녕히 계세요[가세요].	ko·map·sŭm·ni·da an·nyŏng·hi kye·se·yo [ka·se·yo]

Dissatisfied

Can you exchange this, please?	이것을 바꿔 주세요.	i·gŏ·sŭl pa·kwŏ chu·se·yo
I want to return this.	이것을 무르고 싶읍니다.	i·gŏ·sŭl mu·rŭ·go ship·sŭm·ni·da
I'd like a refund. Here's the receipt.	돈을 돌려 주셨으면 좋겠읍니다. 이것이 영수증입니다.	ton·ŭl tol·lyŏ chu·syŏ·ssŭ·myŏn cho·k'e·ssŭm·ni·da i·gŏ·shi yŏng·su·jŭng·im·ni·da

---

You may hear . . .

어서 오세요.	Can I help you?
무엇을 찾으십니까?	What would you like?
어떤 …을 원하십니까?	What . . . would you like?
색깔/모양	colour/shape
질/양	quality/quantity
미안합니다, 없는데요.	I'm sorry, we haven't any.
주문해 드릴까요?	Shall we order it for you?
직접 가지고 가시겠읍니까, 배달해 드릴까요?	Will you take it with you or shall we send it?
이것은 …원입니다.	That's . . . wŏn, please.
…은 받지 않습니다.	We don't accept . . .
크레딧카드	credit cards
여행자 수표	traveller's cheques
당좌 수표	personal cheques

Bookshop—Stationer's—Newsstand

In Korea, bookshops and stationer's are usually separate shops.
Newspapers and magazines are sold at kiosks.

Where's the nearest ...?	가장 가까운 …은 어디입니까?	ka·jang ka·ka·un . . . ŭn ŏ·di·im·ni·ka
bookshop	서점	sŏ·jŏm
stationer's	문방구점	mun·bang·gu·jŏm
newsstand	신문 매점	shin·mun mae·jŏm
Where can I buy an English-language newspaper?	영자 신문은 어디 가면 살 수 있읍니까?	yŏng·ja·shin·mun·ŭn ŏ·di ka·myŏn sal·su i·ssŭm·ni·ka
I want to buy a/an/ some . . .	…을 사고 싶은데요.	. . . ŭl sa·go shi·p'ŭn·de·yo
address book	주소록	chu·so·rok
ballpoint pen	볼펜	pol·p'en
book	책	ch'aek
carbon paper	카본지	k'a·bon·ji
cellophane tape	스카치 테이프	sŭ·k'a·ch'i t'e·i·p'ŭ
crayons	크레용	k'ŭ·re·yong
dictionary	사전	sa·jŏn
Korean-English	한영	han·yŏng
English-Korean	영한	yŏng·han
pocket dictionary	포켓 사전	p'o·k'et sa·jŏn
drawing paper	도화지	to·hwa·ji
elastic bands	고무 밴드	ko·mu baen·dŭ
envelopes	봉투	pong·t'u
eraser	지우개	chi·u·gae
file	파일	p'a·il
fountain pen	만년필	man·nyŏn·p'il
glue	풀	p'ul
grammar book	문법책	mun·bŏp·ch'aek
guide book	안내서	an·nae·sŏ
ink	잉크	ing·k'ŭ
black/red/blue	검정／빨강／청색	kŏm·jŏng／pal·gang／ch'ŏng·saek
labels	레테르	re·t'e·rŭ
magazine	잡지	chap·chi
map	지도	chi·do
map of the town	시가지 지도	shi·ga·ji chi·do
road map	도로 지도	to·ro chi·do

newspaper	신문	shin·mun
American/English	미국의/영국의	mi·guk·ŭi/yŏng·guk·ŭi
notebook	공책	kong·ch'aek
note paper	편지지	p'yŏn·ji·ji
paperback	문고본	mun·go·bon
paper napkins	종이 냅킨	chong·i naep·k'in
paste	풀	p'ul
pen	펜	p'en
pencil	연필	yŏn·p'il
playing cards	트럼프	t'ŭ·rŏm·p'ŭ
postcards	엽서	yŏp·sŏ
refill (for a pen)	(볼펜)심	(pol·p'en) shim
rubber bands	고무 밴드	ko·mu baen·dŭ
Scotch tape	스카치 테이프	sŭ·k'a·ch'i t'e·i·p'ŭ
sketching block	스케치 북	sŭ·k'e·ch'i puk
stamps	우표	u·p'yo
string	끈	kŭn
typewriter ribbon	타자기 리본	t'a·ja·gi ri·bon
typing paper	타이프 용지	t'a·i·p'ŭ yong·ji
wrapping paper	포장지	p'o·jang·ji
Where's the guide-book section?	안내서 파는 데가 어딥니까?	an·nae·sŏ p'a·nŭn te·ga ŏ·dim·ni·ka
Where do you keep the English books?	영어책은 어디 있읍니까?	yŏng·ŏ·ch'aek·ŭn ŏ·di i·ssŭm·ni·ka
Is there an English translation of ...?	...을 영어로 번역한 것이 있읍니까?	... ŭl yŏng·ŏ·ro pŏn·yŏk·han kŏ·shi i·ssŭm·ni·ka

Here are some modern Korean authors whose books are available in English translation.

Kim, Tong-ni	Oh, Young-soo
Hwang, Sun-won	Kim, Young-ik
Choi, Chong-hee	Ha, Tae-heung
Kang, Young-kil	Soh, Chong-joo

Chemist's (pharmacy)—Drugstore

Korean chemist's normally stock a range of goods as wide as the one you find at home. All major cities have excellent stores and some offer round-the-clock service.

For reading ease, this section has been divided into two parts:

1. Pharmaceutical—medicine, first-aid, etc.
2. Toiletry—toilet articles, cosmetics

General

American/English		
Where's the nearest (all-night) chemist's?	가장 가까운 (철야로 영업하는) 약국은 어디에 있읍니까?	ka·jang ka·ka·un (ch'ŏl·ya·ro yŏng·ŏp·ha·nŭn) yak·kuk·ŭn ŏ·di·e i·ssŭm·ni·ka
Can you recommend a good chemist's?	좋은 약국을 가르쳐 주시겠읍니까?	cho ŭn yak·kuk·ŭl ka·rŭ·ch'yŏ chu·shi·ge·ssŭm·ni·ka
What time does the chemist's open?	약국은 몇시에 문을 엽니까?	yak·kuk·ŭn myŏt·shi·e mun·ŭl yŏm·ni·ka
When does the chemist's close?	약국은 몇시에 문을 닫습니까?	yak·kuk·ŭn myŏt·shi·e mun·ŭl ta·ssŭm·ni·ka

Part 1—Pharmaceutical

I want something for . . .	…에 듣는 약을 사고 싶은데요.	. . . e tŭn·nŭn yak·ŭl sa·go shi·p'ŭn·de·yo
a cold/a cough	감기/기침	kam·gi/ki·ch'im
hay fever	건초열	kŏn·ch'o·yŏl
a hangover	숙취	suk·ch'wi
sunburn	햇볕에 탄 데	haet·pyŏt'e t'an te
travel sickness	(차)멀미	(ch'a) mŏl·mi
Can you make up this prescription for me?	이 처방을 조제해 주시겠읍니까?	i ch'ŏ·bang·ŭl cho·je·hae chu·shi·ge·ssŭm·ni·ka
Shall I wait?	기다릴까요?	ki·da·ril·ka·yo
When shall I come back?	언제 다시 올까요?	ŏn·je ta·shi ol·ka·yo

FOR DOCTOR, see page 162

Can I get it without a prescription?	처방이 없어도 받을 수 있읍니까?	ch'ŏ·bang·i ŏp·sŏ·do pa·dŭl·su i·ssŭm·ni·ka
Can I have a/an/some . . . ?	…을 주시겠어요?	. . . ŭl chu·shi·ge·ssŏ·yo

Alka Seltzer	알카 셀처	al·k'a sel·ch'ŏ
antiseptic cream	소독 크림	so·dok k'ŭ·rim
aspirin	아스피린	a·sŭ·p'i·rin
bandage	붕대	pung·dae
Band-Aids	반창고	pan·ch'ang·go
chlorine tablets	염소 타블렛	yŏm·so t'a·bŭl·let
contraceptives	피임약	p'i·im·yak
corn plasters	티눈 고약	t'i·nun ko·yak
cotton wool	탈지면	t'al·chi·myŏn
cough lozenges	기침약(알약)	ki·ch'im·yak (al·yak)
diabetic lozenges	사카린 정제	sa·k'a·rin chŏng·je
disinfectant	소독약	so·dong·nyak
ear drops	귀약	kwi·yak
Elastoplast	반창고	pan·ch'ang·go
eye drops	안약	an·yak
first-aid kit	구급약 상자	ku·gŭp·yak sang·ja
gargle	목 가시는 약	mok ka·shi·nŭn yak
gauze	가제	ka·je
insect lotion	벌레 물린 데 바르는 약	pŏl·le mul·lin·de pa·rŭ·nŭn yak
insect repellent	살충제	sal·ch'ung·je
iodine	옥도정기	ok·do·jŏng·gi
iron pills	철소제	ch'ŏl·so·je
laxative	하제	ha·je
lint	린트천	rin·t'ŭ·ch'ŏn
mouthwash	양치물약	yang·ch'i·mul·yak
quinine tablets	키니네 정제	k'i·ni·ne chŏng·je
sanitary napkins	생리대	saeng·ni·dae
sedative	진정제	chin·jŏng·je
sleeping pills	수면제	su·myŏn·je
stomach pills	위장약	wi·jang·yak
thermometer	체온계	ch'e·on·gye
throat lozenges	인후 정제	in·hu chŏng·je
tissues	화장지	hwa·jang·ji
tranquilizers	신경 안정제	shin·gyŏng an·jŏng·je
vitamin pills	비타민제	pi·t'a·min·je
weight-reducing tablets	체중 줄이는 약	ch'e·jung chu·ri·nŭn yak

Part 2—Toiletry

I'd like a/an/some . . .	…을 주세요.	. . . ŭl chu·se·yo
acne-cream	여드름 크림	yŏ·dŭ·rŭm k'ŭ·rim
after-shave lotion	면도후에 바르는 로션	myŏn·do·hu·e pa·rŭ·nŭn ro·syŏn
bath cubes	바스 큐브	ba·sŭ k'yu·bŭ
bath essence	바스 에쎈스	ba·sŭ e·ssen·sŭ
bath salts	바스 솔트	ba·sŭ sol·t'ŭ
cream	크림	k'ŭ·rim
cleansing cream	클린싱 크림	k'ŭl·lin·sing k'ŭ·rim
cold cream	콜드 크림	k'ol·dŭ k'ŭ·rim
cuticle cream	큐티클 크림	k'yu·t'i·k'ŭl k'ŭ·rim
foundation cream	파운데이션 크림	p'a·un·de·i·syŏn k'ŭ·rim
hormone cream	호르몬 크림	ho·rŭ·mon k'ŭ·rim
moisturizing cream	모이스처링 크림	mo·i·sŭ·ch'yŏ·ring k'ŭ·rim
night cream	나이트 크림	na·i·t'ŭ k'ŭ·rim
cuticle remover	큐티클 리무버	k'yu·t'i·k'ŭl ri·mu·bŏ
deodorant	방취제	pang·ch'wi·je
spray/roll-on	스프레이/롤온	sŭ·p'ŭ·re·i/rol·on
eau de Cologne	오 드 콜론	o tŭ k'ol·lon
emery board	손톱 줄	son·t'op chul
eye liner	아이 라이너	a·i ra·i·nŏ
eye pencil	아이 펜슬	a·i p'en·sŭl
eye shadow	아이 섀도우	a·i sye·do·u
face pack	팩	p'aek
face powder	분	pun
foot cream	풋 크림	p'ut k'ŭ·rim
hand cream	핸드 크림	haen·dŭ k'ŭ·rim
lipstick	립스틱	rip·sŭ·t'ik
lipstick brush	립스틱 브러시	rip·sŭ·t'ik bŭ·rŏ·shi
make-up bag	화장품 백	hwa·jang·p'um paek
make-up remover pads	화장 지우는 패드	hwa·jang chi·u·nŭn p'ae·dŭ
nail brush	손톱솔	son·t'op·sol
nail clippers	손톱깎이	son·t'op·ka·ki
nail file	손톱 다듬는 줄	son·t'op ta·dŭm·nŭn chul
nail lacquer	매니큐어	mae·ni·k'yu·ŏ
nail lacquer remover	매니큐어 지우개	mae·ni·k'yu·ŏ chi·u·gae
nail polish	매니큐어	mae·ni·k'yu·ŏ
nail scissors	손톱가위	son·t'op ka·wi

perfume	향수	hyang·su
powder	분	pun
razor	면도칼	myŏn·do·k'al
razor blades	면도날	myŏn·do·nal
rouge	입술연지	ip·sul·yŏn·ji
safety pins	안전핀	an·jŏn·p'in
shampoo	샴푸	syam·p'u
shaver	전기 면도기	chŏn·gi myŏn·do·gi
shaving brush	면도솔	myŏn·do·sol
shaving cream	면도 크림	myŏn·do k'ŭ·rim
shaving soap	면도 비누	myŏn·do pi·nu
soap	비누	pi·nu
sponge	스폰지	sŭ·p'on·ji
suntan cream	선탠 크림	sŏn·t'aen k'ŭ·rim
suntan oil	선탠 오일	sŏn·t'aen o·il
tissues	화장용지	hwa·jang·yong·ji
toilet bag	화장품 주머니	hwa·jang·p'um chu·mŏ·ni
toilet paper	화장지	hwa·jang·ji
toothbrush	칫솔	ch'i·ssol
toothpaste	치약	ch'i·yak
towel	수건	su·gŏn
tweezers	족집게	chok·chip·ke

For your hair

brush	헤어브러시	he·ŏ·bŭ·rŏ·shi
colouring	머리염색	mŏ·ri yŏm·saek
comb	머리빗	mŏ·ri·bit
curlers	컬 클립	k'ŏl k'ŭl·lip
dye	물감	mul·gam
grips (bobby pins)	헤어그립	he·ŏ·gŭ·rip
lacquer	헤어래커	he·ŏ·rae·k'ŏ
pins	핀	p'in
rollers	롤러	rol·lŏ
setting lotion	세트용 로션	se·t'ŭ·yong ro·syŏn

Clothing

If you want to buy something specific, prepare yourself in advance. Look at the list of clothing on page 113. Get some idea of the colour, material and size you want. They are all listed in the next few pages.

General

I'd like ...	···을 주세요.	... ŭl chu·se·yo
I want ... for a 10-year-old boy.	열살난 사내아이용의 ···을 원하는데요.	yŏl·sal·nan sa·nae·a·i·yong·ŭi ... ŭl wŏn·ha·nŭn·de·yo
I want something like this.	이런 것을 원하는데요.	i·rŏn kŏ·sŭl wŏn·ha·nŭn·de·yo
I like the one in the window.	쇼윈도에 있는 것이 마음에 듭니다.	syo·win·do·e in·nŭn kŏ·shi ma·ŭm·e tŭm·ni·da
How much is that per metre?	1 미터에 얼마입니까?	il·mi·t'ŏ·e ŏl·ma·im·ni·ka

1 centimetre = 0.39 in.	1 inch = 2.54 cm.
1 metre = 39.37 in.	1 foot = 30.5 cm.
10 metres = 32.81 ft.	1 yard = 0.91 m.

Colour

I want something in ...	···한 것을 원합니다.	... han kŏ·sŭl wŏn·ham·ni·da
I want a darker shade.	색깔이 더 짙은 것을 원합니다.	saek·ka·ri tŏ chi·t'ŭn kŏ·sŭl wŏn·ham·ni·da
I want something to match this.	여기에 어울리는 것을 원합니다.	yŏ·gi·e ŏ·ul·li·nŭn kŏ·sŭl wŏn·ham·ni·da
I don't like the colour.	색깔이 마음에 안듭니다.	saek·ka·ri ma·ŭm·e an·dŭm·ni·da

beige	베이지	be·i·ji
black	검정	kŏm·jŏng
blue	청색	ch'ŏng·saek
brown	갈색	kal·saek
cream	크림색	k'ŭ·rim·saek
crimson	심홍색	shim·hong·saek
emerald	에메랄드 그린	e·me·ral·tŭ kŭ·rin
fawn	황갈색	hwang·gal·saek
gold	금빛	kŭm·bit
green	녹색	nok·saek
grey	회색	hoe·saek
mauve	연한 자주빛	yŏn·han cha·ju·bit
orange	오렌지색	o·ren·ji·saek
pink	분홍	pun·hong
purple	자주빛	cha·ju·bit
red	빨강	pal·gang
scarlet	주홍색	chu·hong·saek
silver	은빛	ŭn·bit
tan	황갈색	hwang·gal·saek
white	흰색	hŭin·saek
yellow	노랑	no·rang

줄무늬
(chul·mu·nŭi)

물방울 무늬
(mul·bang·ul·mu·nŭi)

바둑판 무늬
(pa·duk·p'an·mu·nŭi)

연속 무늬
(yŏn·sok·mu·nŭi)

Material

Have you anything in . . . ?	…한 것이 있읍니까?	. . . han kŏ·shi i·ssŭm·ni·ka
I want a cotton blouse.	면블라우스를 원하는데 요.	myŏn·bŭl·la·u·sŭ·rŭl wŏn·ha·nŭn·de·yo
Is that made here ?	그것은 한국제입니까?	kŭ·gŏ·sŭn han·guk·che·im·ni·ka
handmade	수제의	su·je·ŭi
imported	수입한	su·ip·han
I want something thinner.	좀 더 얇은 것을 원합니 다.	chom tŏ yal·bŭn kŏ·sŭl wŏn·ham·ni·da

| Have you any better quality? | 더 좋은 것은 없읍니까? | tŏ cho·ŭn kŏ·sŭn ŏp·sŭm·ni·ka |
| What's it made of? | 천은 무엇입니까? | ch'ŏn·ŭn mu·ŏ·shim·ni·ka |

It may be made of ...

camel-hair	낙타털	nak·t'a·t'ŏl
chiffon	시퐁	shi·p'ong
corduroy	고르뎅	ko·rŭ·deng
cotton	무명	mu·myŏng
felt	펠트	p'el·t'ŭ
flannel	플란넬	p'ŭl·lan·nel
gabardine	개버딘	kae·bŏ·din
lace	레이스	re·i·sŭ
leather	가죽	ka·juk
linen	린네르	rin·ne·rŭ
nylon	나일론	na·il·lon
pique	피케	p'i·k'e
poplin	포플린	p'o·p'ŭl·lin
rayon	레용	re·yong
rubber	고무	ko·mu
satin	공단	kong·dan
serge	사지	sa·ji
silk	명주	myŏng·ju
suede	스웨이드 가죽	sŭ·we·i·dŭ ka·juk
towelling	타월천	t'a·wŏl·ch'ŏn
tulle	명주 망사	myŏng·ju mang·sa
tweed	트위드	t'ŭ·wi·dŭ
velvet	벨벳	pel·bet
wool	양털	yang·t'ŏl
worsted	소모사	so·mo·sa

Size

My size is 38.	내 사이즈는 38 입니다.	nae sa·i·jŭ·nŭn 38 im·ni·da
Our sizes are different at home. Could you measure me?	나라에 따라 사이즈가 다르니까, 재어 주시겠어요?	na·ra·e ta·ra sa·i·jŭ·ga ta·rŭ·ni·ka chae·ŏ chu·shi·ge·ssŏ·yo
I don't know the Korean sizes.	한국 사이즈는 모르겠읍니다.	han·guk sa·i·jŭ·nŭn mo·rŭ·ge·ssŭm·ni·da

In that case, look at the charts on the next page.

This is your size

Ladies

Dresses/suits					
American	8	10	12	14	16	18
British	32/10	34/12	36/14	38/16	40/18	42/20
Korean	43	44	45	46	47	48

Stockings					Shoes			
American	8	$8\frac{1}{2}$	9	$9\frac{1}{2}$	10	6	7	8	9
British						$4\frac{1}{2}$	$5\frac{1}{2}$	$6\frac{1}{2}$	$7\frac{1}{2}$
Korean		One size				$22\frac{1}{2}$	23	$23\frac{1}{2}$	24

Gentlemen

Suits/overcoats						Shirts			
American British	36	38	40	42	44	46	15	16	17	18
Korean	36	37	38	39	40	41	$14\frac{1}{2}$	15	$15\frac{1}{2}$	16

Shoes										
American British	5	6	7	8	$8\frac{1}{2}$	9	$9\frac{1}{2}$	10	11
Korean	$24\frac{1}{2}$	25	$25\frac{1}{2}$	26	$26\frac{1}{2}$	27			

SHOPPING GUIDE

A good fit ?

Can I try it on ?	입어봐도 됩니까 ?	i·bŏ·bwa·do toem·ni·ka
Where's the fitting room ?	착의실은 어디입니까 ?	ch'ak·ŭi·shi·rŭn ŏ·di·im·ni·ka
Is there a mirror ?	거울이 있읍니까 ?	kŏ·u·ri i·ssŭm·ni·ka
Does it fit ?	잘 맞습니까 ?	chal ma·ssŭm·ni·ka

FOR NUMBERS, see page 175

It fits very well.	꼭 맞습니다.	kok ma·ssŭm·ni·da
It doesn't fit.	맞지 않습니다.	mat·ji an·sŭm·ni·da
It's too ...	그건 너무 ...	kŭ·gŏn nŏ·mu ...
short/long/tight/ loose	짧아요/길어요/꼭 껴요/ 헐렁해요	chal·ba·yo/ki·rŏ·yo/kok kyŏ·yo/hŏl·lŏng·hae·yo
How long will it take to alter?	고치는 데 시간이 얼마나 걸립니까?	ko·ch'i·nŭn te shi·gan·i ŏl·ma·na kŏl·lim·ni·ka

Shoes

I'd like a pair of ...	...을 한 켤레 주세요.	...ŭl han k'yŏl·le chu·se·yo
shoes/sandals/boots	구두/샌들/장화	ku·du/saen·dŭl/chang·hwa
These are too ...	이것은 너무...	i·gŏ·sŭn nŏ·mu...
narrow/wide	좁습니다/넓습니다	cho·sŭm·ni·da / nŏl·sŭm·ni·da
large/small	큽니다/작습니다	k'ŭm·ni·da/chak·sŭm·ni·da
Do you have a larger size?	더 큰 사이즈는 없습니까?	tŏ k'ŭn sa·i·jŭ·nŭn ŏp·sŭm·ni·ka
I want a smaller size.	더 작은 사이즈로 주세요.	tŏ cha·gŭn sa·i·jŭ·ro chu·se·yo
Do you have the same in ...?	...으로 같은 것이 있습니까?	...ŭ·ro ka·t'ŭn kŏ·shi i·ssŭm·ni·ka
brown/beige	갈색/베이지색	kal·saek/be·i·ji·saek
black/white	검정색/흰색	kŏm·jŏng·saek/hŭin·saek

Shoes worn out? Here's the key to getting them fixed again.

Can you repair these shoes?	이 구두를 고쳐 주시겠어 요?	i ku·du·rŭl ko·ch'yŏ· chu·shi·ge·ssŏ·yo
Can you stitch this?	이것을 꿰매 주시겠어 요?	i·gŏ·sŭl kwe·mae chu· shi·ge·ssŏ·yo
I want new soles and heels.	창과 뒤축을 갈려고 하는 데요.	ch'ang·gwa twi·ch'u·gŭl kal·lyŏ·go ha·nŭn·de·yo
When will they be ready?	언제쯤 될까요?	ŏn·je·chŭm toel·ka·yo

Clothes and accessories

I would like a/an/	…을 주세요.	…ŭl chu·se·yo
some …		
anorak	아노락	a·no·rak
bathing cap	수영모	su·yŏng·mo
bathing suit	수영복	su·yŏng·bok
bath robe	화장복	hwa·jang·bok
bikini	비키니	bi·k'i·ni
blazer	블레이저 코트	bŭl·le·i·jŏ k'o·t'ŭ
blouse	블라우스	bŭl·la·u·sŭ
bolero	볼레로	bol·le·ro
bow tie	나비 넥타이	na·bi nek·t'a·i
bra	브라자	bŭ·ra·ja
braces (Br.)	바지 멜빵	pa·ji mel·pang
cap	모자	mo·ja
cape	케이프	k'e·i·p'ŭ
cardigan	카디간	k'a·di·gan
coat	상의	sang·ŭi
costume	수트	su·t'ŭ
dinner jacket	턱시도	t'ŏk·si·do
dress	드레스	dŭ·re·sŭ
dressing gown	화장복	hwa·jang·bok
evening dress	이브닝 드레스	i·bŭ·ning dŭ·re·sŭ
(woman's)		
dungarees	덩거리 바지	tŏng·gŏ·ri pa·ji
frock	드레스	dŭ·re·sŭ
fur coat	모피 코트	mo·p'i k'o·t'ŭ
girdle	거들	kŏ·dŭl
gloves	장갑	chang·gap
handkerchief	손수건	son·su·gŏn
hat	모자	mo·ja
housecoat	실내복	shil·nae·bok
jacket	자켓	cha·k'et
jeans	진 바지	chin pa·ji
jersey	져지	chyŏ·ji
jumper (Br.)	잠바	cham·ba
hanbok	한복	han·bok
knickers	반바지	pan·ba·ji
lingerie	란제리	ran·je·ri
necktie	넥타이	nek·t'a·i
nightdress	잠옷	cham·ot

overcoat	외투	oe·t'u
pullover	풀오버	p'ul·o·bŏ
pyjamas	파자마	p'a·ja·ma
raincoat	비옷	pi·ot
robe	원피스	wŏn·p'i·sŭ
rubber boots	고무 장화	ko·mu chang·hwa
sandals	샌들	saen·dŭl
scarf	스카프	sŭ·k'a·p'ŭ
shirt	와이샤쓰	wa·i·sya·ssŭ
shoes	구두	ku·du
shorts (Br.)	쇼트 팬츠	syo·t'ŭ p'aen·ch'ŭ
skirt	스커트	sŭ·k'ŏ·t'ŭ
slacks	슬랙스	sŭl·lek·sŭ
slip	슬립	sŭl·lip
slippers	슬리퍼	sŭl·li·p'ŏ
sneakers	운동화	un·dong·hwa
socks	양말	yang·mal
sports jacket	스포츠 자켓	sŭ·p'o·ch'ŭ cha·k'et
stockings	스타킹	sŭ·t'a·k'ing
suit (men's)	신사복	shin·sa·bok
suspenders	바지 멜빵	pa·ji mel·pang
sweater	스웨터	sŭ·we·t'ŏ
T-shirt	티샤쓰	t'i·sya·ssŭ
tennis shoes	정구화	chŏng·gu·hwa
tie	넥타이	nek·t'a·i
top coat	토퍼	t'o·p'ŏ
trousers	양복 바지	yang·bok pa·ji
underpants (men)	팬츠	p'aen·ch'ŭ

belt	허리띠	hŏ·ri·ti
buckle	버클	bŏ·k'ŭl
button	단추	tan·ch'u
collar	깃	kit
cuffs	커프스	k'ŏ·p'ŭ·sŭ
elastic	고무	ko·mu
hem	옷단	ot·dan
lapel	접은 깃	chŏ·bŭn kit
lining	안감	an·gam
pocket	포켓	p'o·k'et
ribbon	리본	ri·bon
sleeve	소매	so·mae
zip(per)	지퍼	chi·p'ŏ

Electrical appliances and accessories—Records

In Korea, both 110 and 220 volt AC are used, with 60 cycles nation-wide. Sockets (outlets) include watts or kilowatts; where KVA is used, 1 KVA is equivalent to 1 kilowatt.

I want a plug for this ...	이 …에 쓰는 플러그가 있읍니까?	i ... e ssŭ-nŭn p'ŭl-lŏ-gŭ-ga i-ssŭm-ni-ka
Have you a battery for this ... ?	이 …에 쓰는 전지가 있읍니까?	i ... e ssŭ-nŭn chŏn-ji-ga i-ssŭm-ni-ka
This is broken. Can you repair it?	이것이 고장났어요. 고쳐 주실 수 있읍니까?	i-gŏ-shi ko-jang-na-ssŏ-yo ko-ch'yŏ chu-shil-su i-ssŭm-ni-ka
When will it be ready?	언제 됩니까?	ŏn-je toem-ni-ka
I'd like a/an/ some ...	…을 주세요.	... ŭl chu-se-yo
adaptor	아답타	a-dap-t'a
amplifier	앰프	aem-p'ŭ
battery	전지	chŏn-ji
cassette	카셋트	k'a-set-t'ŭ
clock	시계	shi-gye
wall clock	벽시계	pyŏk-shi-gye
electronic calculator	전자 계산기	chŏn-ja kye-san-gi
food mixer	믹서기	mik-sŏ-gi
hair-dryer	헤어 드라이어	he-ŏ dŭ-ra-i-ŏ
headset	헤드폰	he-dŭ-p'on
iron	다리미	ta-ri-mi
microphone	마이크로폰	ma-i-k'ŭ-ro-p'on
percolator	커피 끓이개	k'ŏ-p'i kŭ-ri-gae
plug	플러그	p'ŭl-lŏ-gŭ
radio	라디오	ra-di-o
car radio	자동차용 라디오	cha-dong-ch'a-yong ra-di-o
portable radio	휴대용 라디오	hyu-dae-yong ra-di-o
record	레코드	re-k'o-dŭ
record player	전축	chŏn-ch'uk
portable record player	휴대용 전축	hyu-dae-yong chŏn-ch'uk
shaver	전기면도기	chŏn-gi myŏn-do-gi
speakers	스피커	sŭ-p'i-k'ŏ

tape recorder	테이프 레코더	t'e·i·p'ŭ re·k'o·dŏ
cassette tape recorder	카셋트 테이프 레코더	k'a·set·t'ŭ t'e·i·p'ŭ re·k'o·dŏ
portable tape recorder	휴대용 테이프 레코더	hyu·dae·yong t'e·i·p'ŭ re·k'o·dŏ
television	텔레비젼	t'el·le·bi·jyŏn
colour television	칼라 텔레비젼	k'al·la t'el·le·bi·jyŏn
portable television	휴대용 텔레비젼	hyu·dae·yong t'el·le·bi·jyŏn
toaster	토스터	t'o·sŭ·t'ŏ

Record shop

Have you any records by . . . ?	…의 레코드가 있읍니까?	. . . ŭi re·k'o·dŭ·ga i·ssŭm·ni·ka ?
Can I listen to this record ?	이 레코드를 들어볼 수 있읍니까?	i re·k'o·dŭ·rŭl tŭ·rŏ·bol su i·ssŭm·ni·ka
I want a new needle.	새 바늘을 하나 주세요.	sae pa·nŭ·rŭl ha·na chu·se·yo

L.P.	엘피	el·p'i
33/45rpm	33/45 회전	sam·ship·sam/sa·ship·o hoe·jŏn
mono/stereo	모노/스테레오	mo·no/sŭ·t'e·re·o

classical music	클래식 음악	k'ŭl·lae·shik ŭm·ak
folk music	민요	min·yo
instrumental music	기악	ki·ak
jazz	재즈	chae·jŭ
light music	경음악	kyŏng·ŭm·ak
orchestral music	관현악	kwan·hyŏn·ak
pop music	팝 뮤직	p'ap myu·jik

Here are the names of a few popular recording artists known throughout Korea.

Cho, Yong-pil	Cho, Young-nam	Choi, Jin-hee
Kim, Su-hee	Patty Kim	Na-mi
Song, Chang-shik	Kim, Yon-ja	Chong, Su-ra
Lee, Mi-ja	Lee, Eun-ha	Hae-ba-ra-gi (Duo)
Kim, Su-chol	Hye-eun-i	Song-gol-mae (Band)
Yun, Shi-nae	Ku, Chang-mo	San-ul-lim (Band)

Equipment

Here we're concerned with the equipment you may need when camping, picnicking or on excursions—or for just one of those odd situations when one needs something rather unusual . . .

I'd like a/an/ some . . .	…을 주세요.	… ŭl chu·se·yo
axe	도끼	to·ki
bottle-opener	마개따개	ma·gae·ta·gae
bucket	바께쓰	ba·ke·ssŭ
butane gas	부탄 가스	bu·t'an ka·sŭ
camp bed	캠프용 침대	k'aem·p'ŭ·yong ch'im·dae
camping equipment	캠핑 장비	k'aem·p'ing chang·bi
can opener	깡통따개	kang·t'ong·ta·gae
candles	양초	yang·ch'o
chair	의자	ŭi·ja
folding chair	접는 의자	chŏp·nŭn ŭi·ja
compass	자석	cha·sŏk
corkscrew	마개뽑이	ma·gae·po·bi
crockery	오지그릇	o·ji·gŭ·rŭt
cutlery	식탁용 나이프	shik·t'ak·yong na·i·p'ŭ
deck chair	갑판 의자	kap·p'an ŭi·ja
first-aid kit	구급약 상자	ku·gŭp·yak sang·ja
fishing tackle	낚시 도구	nak·shi to·gu
flashlight	플래시	p'ŭl·lae·shi
frying pan	프라이팬	p'ŭ·ra·i·p'aen
groundsheet	방수 깔개	pang·su kal·gae
hammer	망치	mang·ch'i
hammock	해먹	hae·mŏk
haversack	잡낭	chap·nang
ice-bag	얼음 주머니	ŏ·rŭm chu·mŏ·ni
kerosene	등유	tŭng·yu
kettle	주전자	chu·jŏn·ja
knapsack	배낭	pae·nang
lamp	램프	raem·p'ŭ
lantern	랜턴	raen·t'ŏn
matches	성냥	sŏng·nyang
mattress	매트레스	mae·t'ŭ·re·sŭ
mosquito net	모기장	mo·gi·jang
pail	바께쓰	ba·ke·ssŭ

paraffin	등유	tŭng·yu
penknife	주머니칼	chu·mŏ·ni·k'al
picnic case	피크닉 자루	p'i·k'ŭ·nik cha·ru
pressure cooker	압력솥	am·nyŏk·sot
primus stove	휴대용 석유 난로	hyu·dae·yong sŏ·gyu nal·lo
rope	밧줄	pat·jul
rucksack	배낭	pae·nang
saucepan	스튜 남비	sŭ·t'yu nam·bi
scissors	가위	ka·wi
screwdriver	나사돌리개	na·sa·dol·li·gae
sheath-knife	칼집이 있는 칼	k'al·ji·bi in·nŭn k'al
sleeping bag	침낭	ch'im·nang
stewpan	스튜 남비	sŭ·t'yu nam·bi
stove	난로	nal·lo
table	테이블	t'e·i·bŭl
folding table	접는 테이블	chŏm·nŭn t'e·i·bŭl
tent	천막	ch'ŏn·mak
tent peg	천막 말뚝	ch'ŏn·mak mal·tuk
tent-pole	천막 기둥	ch'ŏn·mak ki·dung
thermos flask (bottle)	보온병	po·on·byŏng
tin-opener	깡통따개	kang·t'ong·ta·gae
tongs	부젓가락	pu·jŏt·ga·rak
tool kit	연장통	yŏn·jang·t'ong
torch	회중 전등	hoe·jung chŏn·dŭng
vacuum flask	진공 보온병	chin·gong po·on·byŏng
water carrier	휴대용 물통	hyu·dae·yong mul·t'ong

Crockery

beakers	유리컵	yu·ri·k'ŏp
cups	찻잔	ch'at·jan
mugs	원통형 찻잔	wŏn·t'ong·hyŏng ch'at·jan
plates	접시	chŏp·shi
saucers	받침 접시	pa·ch'im chŏp·shi

Cutlery

forks	포크	p'o·k'ŭ
knives	나이프	na·i·p'ŭ
spoons	스푼	sŭ·p'un
teaspoons	찻숟갈	ch'at·su·gal
(made of) plastic	플래스틱 (으로 만든)	p'ŭl·lae·sŭ·t'ik(ŭ·ro man·dŭn)
(made of) stainless steel	스텐레스 (로 만든)	sŭ·t'en·re·sŭ(ro man·dŭn)

Men's hairdressing (barber)

I don't speak much Korean.	한국말은 잘 못합니다.	han·guk·mal·ŭn chal mot·ham·ni·da
I'm in a terrible hurry.	매우 바쁩니다.	mae·u pa·pŭm·ni·da
I want a haircut, please.	머리를 깎아 주세요.	mŏ·ri·rŭl ka·ka chu·se·yo
I'd like a shave.	면도를 해주세요.	myŏn·do·rŭl hae·ju·se·yo
Don't cut it too short.	너무 짧게 깎지 마세요.	nŏ·mu chal·ke kak·chi ma·se·yo
Scissors only, please.	가위로만 해주세요.	ka·wi·ro·man hae·ju·se·yo
A razor-cut, please.	면도칼로 커트해 주세요.	myŏn·do·k'al·lo k'ŏ·t'ŭ·hae chu·se·yo
Don't use the clippers.	이발기로 하지 마세요.	i·bal·gi·ro ha·ji ma·se·yo
Just a trim, please.	대충 다듬어 주세요.	tae·ch'ung ta·dŭm·ŏ chu·se·yo
That's enough off.	그것으로 됐읍니다.	kŭ·gŏ·sŭ·ro twe·ssŭm·ni·da
A little more off the ...	...을 조금 더 깎아 주세요.	...ŭl cho·gŭm tŏ ka·ka chu·se·yo
back	뒤	twi
neck	목부분	mok·pu·bun
sides	옆	yŏp
top	꼭대기	kok·tae·gi
I don't want any cream.	크림은 안발라도 됩니다.	k'ŭ·rim·ŭn an·bal·la·do toem·ni·da
Would you please trim my ...?	...을 좀 다듬어 주시겠어요?	...ŭl chom ta·dŭm·ŏ chu·shi·ge·ssŏ·yo
beard	턱수염	t'ŏk·su·yŏm
moustache	콧수염	k'ot·su·yŏm
sideboards (sideburns)	구레나룻	ku·re·na·rut
Thank you. That's fine.	고맙습니다. 이제 됐읍니다.	ko·map·sŭm·ni·da i·je twe·ssŭm·ni·da
How much do I owe you?	얼맙니까?	ŏl·mam·ni·ka

SHOPPING GUIDE

FOR TIPPING, see page 1

Ladies' hairdressing

Is there a beauty salon in the hotel?	호텔 안에 미장원이 있읍니까?	ho·t'el·an·e mi·jang·wŏn·i i·ssŭm·ni·ka
Can I make an appointment for sometime on Tuesday?	화요일 적당한 시간에 예약을 할 수 있읍니까?	hwa·yo·il chŏk·tang·han shi·gan·e ye·ya·gŭl hal·su i·ssŭm·ni·ka
I'd like it cut and shaped ...	커트를 하고 …으로 해주세요.	k'ŏ·t'ŭ·rŭl ha·go ... ŭ·ro hae·ju·se·yo
with a fringe	이마에 드리운 앞머리	i·ma·e tŭ·ri·un am·mŏ·ri
with ringlets	곱슬머리	kop·sŭl·mŏ·ri
with waves	웨이브	we·i·bŭ
in a bun	묶은 머리	mu·kŭn mŏ·ri
I want a ...	…해 주세요.	... hae·chu·se·yo
bleach	탈색	t'al·saek
colour rinse	컬러 린스	k'ŏl·lŏ rin·sŭ
dye	염색	yŏm·saek
perm(anent)	파마	p'a·ma
shampoo and set	샴푸와 세트	sham·p'u·wa se·t'ŭ
tint	윤내기	yun·nae·gi
touch up	마무리	ma·mu·ri
the same colour	같은 색깔	ka·t'ŭn sae·kal
a darker colour	더 진한 색깔	tŏ chin·han sae·kal
a lighter colour	더 옅은 색깔	tŏ yŏl·bŭn sae·kal
auburn/blond/ brunette	다갈색/블론드/브루넷	ta·gal·saek / bŭl·lon·dŭ / bŭ·ru·net
I want a ...	…을 해주세요.	... ŭl hae·ju·se·yo
manicure/pedicure/ facepack	매니큐어/페디큐어/팩	mae·ni·k'yu·ŏ/p'e·di·k'yu·ŏ/ p'aek

FOR TIPPING, see page 1

SHOPPING GUIDE

Jeweller's—Watchmaker's

Can you repair this watch ?	이 시계를 고쳐 주실 수 있읍니까 ?	i shi·gye·rŭl ko·ch'yŏ chu·shil·su i·ssŭm·ni·ka
The ... is broken.	…이 깨졌어요.	... i kae·jŏ·ssŏ·yo
glass/spring/strap	유리/태엽/밴드	yu·ri/t'ae·yŏp/baen·dŭ
I want this watch cleaned.	이 시계를 분해 소제해 주세요.	i shi·gye·rŭl pun·hae so·je·hae chu·se·yo
When will it be ready ?	언제 될까요 ?	ŏn·je toel·ka·yo
Could I see that, please ?	좀 보여 주시겠어요 ?	chom po·yŏ chu·shi·ge·ssŏ·yo
I'm just looking round.	구경 좀 합니다.	ku·gyŏng chom ham·ni·da
I want a small present for ...	…에게 줄 자그마한 선물을 찾고 있읍니다.	... e·ge chul cha·gŭ·ma·han sŏn·mul·ŭl ch'at·go i·ssŭm·ni·da
I don't want anything too expensive.	너무 값비싼 것은 원치 않습니다.	nŏ·mu kap·pi·ssan kŏ·sŭn wŏn·ch'i an·sŭm·ni·da
I want something ...	…한 것을 원합니다.	... han kŏ·sŭl wŏn·ham·ni·da
better/cheaper/simpler	더 좋은/더 싼/더 간단한	tŏ cho·ŭn/tŏ ssan/tŏ kan·dan·han
Have you anything in gold ?	금으로 된 것이 있읍니까 ?	kŭm·ŭ·ro toen kŏ·shi i·ssŭm·ni·ka
Is this real silver ?	진짜 은입니까 ?	chin·cha ŭn·im·ni·ka

If it's made of gold, ask :

How many dons is this ?	이것은 몇 돈입니까 ?	i·gŏ·sŭn myŏt don·im·ni·ka

Korea is a producer of world-famous amethyst and smoky topaz, and offers a greater variety of these stones than anywhere else in the world. They are among the best at a Korean jeweller's.

SHOPPING GUIDE

When you go to a jeweller's, you've probably got some idea of what you want beforehand. Find out what the article is made of and then look up the Korean name for the article itself in the following lists.

What's it made of?

amber	호박	ho-bak
amethyst	자수정	cha-su-jŏng
chromium	크로뮴	k'ŭ-ro-myum
copper	구리	ku-ri
coral	산호	san-ho
crystal	수정	su-jŏng
cut glass	커트글라스	k'ŏ-t'ŭ-gŭl-la-sŭ
diamond	다이아몬드	da-i-a-mon-dŭ
ebony	흑단	hŭk-tan
emerald	에메랄드	e-me-ral-dŭ
enamel	에나멜	e-na-mel
glass	유리	yu-ri
gold	금	kŭm
gold-leaf	금박	kŭm-bak
ivory	상아	sang-a
jade	비취	pi-ch'wi
onyx	줄마노	chul-ma-no
pearl	진주	chin-ju
pewter	백랍	paeng-nap
platinum	백금	paek-kŭm
ruby	루비	ru-bi
sapphire	사파이어	sa-p'a-i-ŏ
silver	은	ŭn
silver-plate	은도금	ŭn-do-gŭm
stainless steel	스텐레스	sŭ-t'en-re-sŭ
topaz	황옥	hwang-ok
turquoise	터키옥	t'ŏ-k'i-ok

What is it ?

d like a/an/ some ...	…을 주세요.	…ŭl chu·se·yo
bracelet	팔찌	p'al·chi
brooch	브로치	bŭ·ro·ch'i
chain	사슬	sa·sŭl
charm	장식품	chang·shik·p'um
cigarette case	담배 케이스	tam·bae k'e·i·sŭ
cigarette lighter	라이터	ra·i·t'ŏ
clock	시계	shi·gye
cross	십자가	ship·cha·ga
cuff-links	커프스 단추	k'ŏ·p'ŭ·sŭ tan·ch'u
cutlery	식탁용 나이프류	shik·t'ak·yong na·i·p'ŭ·ryu
earrings	귀고리	kwi·go·ri
jewel box	보석상자	po·sŏk sang·ja
manicure set	매니큐어 세트	mae·ni·k'yu·ŏ se·t'ŭ
mechanical pencil	샤프 펜슬	sya·p'ŭ p'en·sŭl
necklace	목걸이	mok·kŏ·ri
pendant	늘어뜨린 장식	nŭ·rŏ·tŭ·rin chang·shik
pin	핀	p'in
powder compact	분첩	pun·ch'ŏp
propelling pencil	샤프 펜슬	sya·p'ŭ p'en·sŭl
ring	반지	pan·ji
engagement ring	약혼 반지	yak·hon pan·ji
wedding ring	결혼 반지	kyŏl·hon pan·ji
rosary	묵주	muk·chu
silverware	은그릇	ŭn·gŭ·rŭt
strap	밴드	baen·dŭ
chain strap	사슬로 된 밴드	sa·sŭl·lo toen baen·dŭ
leather strap	가죽 밴드	ka·juk baen·dŭ
watch strap	시계 밴드	shi·gye baen·dŭ
tie-clip	넥타이 클립	nek·t'a·i k'ŭl·lip
tie-pin	넥타이 핀	nek·t'a·i p'in
vanity case	화장 도구 상자	hwa·jang to·gu sang·ja
watch	시계	shi·gye
pocket watch	회중 시계	hoe·jung shi·gye
with a second-hand	초침이 달린	ch'o·ch'im·i tal·lin
wristwatch	손목 시계	son·mok shi·gye

Laundry — Dry cleaning

If your hotel doesn't have its own laundry/dry cleaning service, ask the porter:

Where's the nearest laundry?	제일 가까운 세탁소가 어 딥니까?	che·il ka·ka·un se·t'ak·so·ga ŏ·dim·ni·ka
I want these clothes ...	이 옷을 … 주세요.	i o·sŭl ... chu·se·yo
cleaned	클리닝해	k'ŭl·li·ning·hae
pressed	프레스해	p'ŭ·re·sŭ·hae
ironed	다려	ta·ryŏ
washed	빨아	pa·ra
When will it be ready?	언제 됩니까?	ŏn·je toem·ni·ka
I need it ...	… 필요합니다.	...p'i·ryo·ham·ni·da
today	오늘	o·nŭl
tonight	오늘밤	o·nŭl·bam
tomorrow	내일	nae·il
before Friday	금요일 전에	kŭm·yo·il chŏn·e
I want it as soon as possible.	될 수 있는 대로 빨리 부 탁합니다.	toel·su in·nŭn·dae·ro pal·li pu·t'ak·ham·ni·da
Can you ... this?	이것을 … 주시겠어요?	i·gŏ·sŭl ... chu·shi·ge·ssŏ·yo
mend/patch/stitch	고쳐/기워/꿰매	ko·ch'yŏ/ki·wŏ/kwe·mae
Can you sew on this button?	이 단추를 달아 주시겠어 요?	i tan·ch'u·rŭl ta·ra chu·shi·ge·ssŏ·yo
Can you get this stain out?	이 얼룩을 뺄 수 있습니까?	i ŏl·lu·gŭl pael·su i·ssŭm·ni·ka
Can this be invisibly mended?	이것을 보이지 않게 기워 주실 수 있어요?	i·gŏ·sŭl po·i·ji an·k'e ki·wŏ chu·shil·su i·ssŏ·yo
This isn't mine.	이것은 나의 것이 아닙니 다.	i·gŏ·sŭn na·ŭi kŏ·shi a·nim·ni·da
Where's my laundry?	나의 세탁물은 어디 있읍 니까?	na·ŭi se·t'ak·mu·rŭn ŏ·di i·ssŭm·ni·ka
You promised it for today.	오늘까지 해준다고 하셨 는데요.	o·nŭl·ka·ji hae·jun·da·go ha·syŏn·nŭn·de·yo

Photography — Cameras

Basic still and home-movie exposures are given in English in the instructions with the roll of film.

I want an inexpensive camera.	값이 싼 카메라를 원합니다.	kap·si ssan k'a·me·ra·rŭl wŏn·ham·ni·da
Show me that one in the window.	쇼원도에 있는 저것을 보여 주세요.	sho·win·do·e in·nŭn chŏ·gŏ·sŭl po·yŏ chu·se·yo

Films

I'd like a ...	...을 원하는데요.	...ŭl wŏn·ha·nŭn·de·yo
film for this camera	이 카메라용 필름	i k'a·me·ra·yong p'il·lŭm
120 (6×6) film	6×6의 필름	yuk nyuk·ŭi p'il·lŭm
126 (26×26) film	26×26의 필름	i·shim·nyuk i·shim·nyuk·ŭi p'il·lŭm
127 (4×4) film	4×4의 필름	sa sa·ŭi p'il·lŭm
135 (24×36) film	24×36의 필름	i·ship·sa sam·shim·nyuk·ŭi p'il·lŭm
126 Instamatic	126 인스터매틱	paek·i·shim·nyuk in·sŭ·t'ŏ·mae·t'ik
8mm film	8밀리 필름	p'al·mil·li p'il·lŭm
super 8	수퍼 8	su·p'ŏ e·i·t'ŭ
16mm film	16밀리 필름	shim·nyuk mil·li p'il·lŭm
35mm film	35밀리 필름	sam·shi·bo mil·li p'il·lŭm
620 (6×6) roll film	가는 축 브로니판 필름	ka·nŭn ch'uk pŭ·ro·ni·p'an p'il·lŭm
20/36 exposures	20/36 감개	i·ship/sam·shim·nyuk kam·gae
this size	이 사이즈	i sa·i·jŭ
this ASA/DIN number	이 필름 감도	i p'il·lŭm kam·do
black and white	흑백	hŭk·paek
colour	칼라	k'al·la
colour negative	칼라 네가	k'al·la ne·ga
colour reversal	칼라 리버설	k'al·la ri·bŏ·sŏl
colour slide (transparency)	칼라 슬라이드	k'al·la sŭl·la·i·dŭ
artificial light type	텅스텐 타이프	t'ŏng·sŭ·t'en t'a·i·p'ŭ
daylight type	데이라이트 타이프	te·i·ra·i·t'ŭ t'a·i·p'ŭ
fast/fine grain	고감도/미립자 필름	ko·gam·do/mi·rip·cha p'il·lŭm
Does this price include processing?	이 가격에는 현상료도 포함되어 있읍니까?	i ka·gyŏk·e·nŭn hyŏn·sang·nyo·do p'o·ham·doe·ŏ i·ssŭm·ni·ka

FOR NUMBERS, see page 175

Processing

How much do you charge for developing?	현상하는 데 얼맙니까?	hyŏn·sang·ha·nŭn·de ŏl·mam·ni·ka
I want ... prints of each negative.	이 네가를 …장씩 인화하고 싶은데요.	i ne·ga·rŭl ...chang·sik in·hwa·ha·go shi·p'ŭn·de·yo
Will you enlarge this, please?	이것을 확대해 주시겠어요?	i·gŏ·sŭl hwak·tae·hae chu·shi·ge·ssŏ·yo

Accessories

I want a/an/some ...	…을 주세요.	...ŭl chu·se·yo
cable release	셔터 릴리즈	shŏ·t'ŏ ril·li·jŭ
exposure meter	노출계	no·ch'ul·gye
flash bulbs	플래시 벌브	p'ŭl·lae·shi bŏl·bŭ
flash cubes	플래시 큐브	p'ŭl·lae·shi k'yu·bŭ
for black and white	흑백용	hŭk·paek·yong
for colour	칼라용	k'al·la·yong
filter	필터	p'il·t'ŏ
red/yellow	빨강/노랑	pal·gang/no·rang
ultra-violet	자외선	cha·oe·sŏn
lens	렌즈	ren·jŭ
lens cap	렌즈 덮개	ren·jŭ tŏp·kae
lens cleaners	렌즈 닦개	ren·jŭ tak·kae
tripod	삼각	sam·gak
zoom lens	줌 렌즈	chum ren·jŭ

Broken

This camera doesn't work. Can you repair it?	이 카메라가 고장났어요. 고쳐 주실 수 있어요?	i k'a·me·ra·ga ko·jang·na·ssŏ·yo. ko·ch'yŏ·chu·shil·su i·ssŏ·yo
The film is jammed.	필름이 돌아가지 않아요.	p'il·lŭm·i to·ra·ga·ji a·na·yo
There's something wrong with the...	이 …이 어딘가 잘못된 것 같아요.	i ...ŏ·din·ga chal·mot·doen kŏt ka·t'a·yo
exposure counter	노출계	no·ch'ul·gye
film winder	필름 감개	p'il·lŭm kam·gae
lightmeter	라이트 미터	ra·i·t'ŭ mi·t'ŏ
rangefinder	레인지 파인더	re·in·ji p'a·in·dŏ
shutter	셔터	shŏ·t'ŏ

Provisions

Here's a list of basic food and drink that you might want on a
picnic or for the occasional meal at home.

I'd like a/an/some...	…을 주세요.	…ŭl chu·se·yo
apples	사과	sa·gwa
bananas	바나나	ba·na·na
biscuits (Br.)	비스켓	bi·sŭ·k'et
bread	빵	pang
butter	버터	bŏ·t'ŏ
cake	케이크	k'e·i·k'ŭ
cheese	치즈	ch'i·jŭ
chocolate	초콜렛	ch'o·k'ol·let
coffee	커피	k'ŏ·p'i
cold meat	냉육	naeng·yuk
cookies	쿠키	k'u·k'i
cooking fat	요리용 지방	yo·ri·yong chi·bang
crackers	크래커	k'ŭ·rae·k'ŏ
crisps (potato chips)	감자 칩	kam·ja ch'ip
cucumbers	오이	o·i
frankfurters	비엔나 소시지	pi·en·na so·shi·ji
ham	햄	haem
hamburgers	햄버거	haem·bŏ·gŏ
ice cream	아이스크림	a·i·sŭ·k'ŭ·rim
lemonade	레모네이드	le·mo·ne·i·dŭ
lemons	레몬	le·mon
lettuce	상치	sang·ch'i
liver sausage	간 소시지	kan so·shi·ji
luncheon meat	콘비프류	k'on·bi·p'ŭ·ryu
milk	우유	u·yu
mustard	겨자	kyŏ·ja
orange squash (drink)	오렌지 스카시	o·ren·ji sŭ·k'a·shi
oranges	오렌지	o·ren·ji
paté	파테	p'a·t'e
pepper	후추	hu·ch'u
pickles	야채 절임	ya·ch'ae chŏ·rim
pork	돼지고기	twe·ji·go·gi
potatoes	감자	kam·ja
rolls	롤빵	rol·pang
salad	샐러드	sael·lŏ·dŭ
salami	살라미	sal·la·mi

sandwiches	샌드위치	saen·dŭ·wi·ch'i
sausages	소시지	so·shi·ji
spaghetti	스파게티	sŭ·p'a·ge·t'i
sugar	설탕	sŏl·t'ang
sweets	과자	kwa·ja
tea	홍차	hong·ch'a
tomatoes	토마토	t'o·ma·t'o

And don't forget...

a bottle opener	병따개	pyŏng·ta·gae
a corkscrew	코르크 마개뽑이	k'o·rŭ·k'ŭ ma·gae·po·bi
matches	성냥	sŏng·nyang
paper napkins	종이 냅킨	chong·i naep·k'in
a tin (can) opener	깡통따개	kang·t'ong·ta·gae

Weights and measures
1 kilogram or kilo (kg) = 1000 grams (g)

| 100 g = 3.5 oz. | $\frac{1}{2}$ kg = 1.1 lb. |
| 200 g = 7.0 oz. | 1 kg = 2.2 lb. |

1 oz. = 28.35 g
1 lb. = 453.60 g

1 litre (l) = 0.88 imp. quarts = 1.06 U.S. quarts

| 1 imp. quart = 1.14 l | 1 U.S. quart = 0.95 l |
| 1 imp. gallon = 4.55 l | 1 U.S. gallon = 3.8 l |

barrel	술통	sul·t'ong
box	상자	sang·ja
can	깡통	kang·t'ong
carton	마분지 상자	ma·bun·ji sang·ja
crate	바구니	pa·gu·ni
jar	단지	tan·ji
packet	꾸러미	ku·rŏ·mi
tin	깡통	kang·t'ong
tube	튜브	t'yu·bŭ

Souvenirs

Korean textiles, particularly those used for clothing (such as the traditional *han·bok*), scarves, decorative materials, bedclothes (bedding), etc., are noted world-wide for their high quality and low price. Costume dolls, wooden tableware, such as wooden bowls, and all types of hand-made products, including finely-woven straw mats and mother-of-pearl inlaid tables, are famous for their superb craftsmanship.

bamboo products	죽세공품	chuk·se·gong·p'um
brocades	비단	pi·dan
cigarette lighters	라이터	ra·i·t'ŏ
cultured pearls	진주	chin·ju
cutlery	식탁용 나이프류	shik·t'ak·yong na·i·p'ŭ·ryu
damask	상감	sang·gam
dolls	인형	in·hyŏng
fans	부채	pu·ch'ae
fishing rods and reels	낚시 도구	nak·shi to·gu
folkcrafts	민예품	min·ye·p'um
handbags	핸드백	haen·dŭ·baek
hanging-picture rolls	족자	chok·cha
hanbok	한복	han·bok
lacquerware	칠기	ch'il·gi
manicure sets	매니큐어 세트	mae·ni·k'yu·ŏ se·t'ŭ
music boxes	음악상자	ŭm·ak·sang·ja
painted screens	병풍	pyŏng·p'ung
paper products	종이 제품	chong·i che·p'um
porcelains	도자기	to·ja·gi
silks	명주	myŏng·ju
woodwork	목공품	mok·gong·p'um
toys	장난감	chang·nan·gam
woodblock prints	목판화	mok·p'an·hwa

Tobacconist's

As elsewhere, cigarettes are generally referred to by their brand names. The best-known Korean cigarettes are *Sol* and *Arirang*.

Buying

Give me a/an/ some... please.	…을 주세요.	...ŭl chu·se·yo
box of...	…을 한 갑	...ŭl han kap
cigar	엽궐련	yŏp·gwŏl·lyŏn
cigarette case	담배 케이스	tam·bae k'e·i·sŭ
cigarette holder	담배 물부리	tam·bae mul·bu·ri
cigarette lighter	라이터	ra·i·t'ŏ
flints	라이터돌	ra·i·t'ŏ·dol
lighter	라이터	ra·i·t'ŏ
lighter fluid/gas	라이터 기름/가스	ra·i·t'ŏ ki·rŭm/ga·sŭ
refill for a lighter	라이터에 기름넣기	ra·i·t'ŏ·e ki·rŭm·nŏ·k'i
matches	성냥	sŏng·nyang
packet of cigarettes	담배 한 갑	tam·bae han kap
packet of...	…을 한 갑	...ŭl han kap
pipe	파이프	p'a·i·p'ŭ
pipe tobacco	파이프 담배	p'a·i·p'ŭ tam·bae
pipe cleaners	파이프 청소기	p'a·i·p'ŭ ch'ŏng·so·gi
tobacco pouch	담배 쌈지	tam·bae ssam·ji
wick	심지	shim·ji
Have you any...?	…이 있읍니까?	...i i·ssŭm·ni·ka
American cigarettes	미국 담배	mi·guk tam·bae
English cigarettes	영국 담배	yŏng·guk tam·bae
matches	성냥	sŏng·nyang
menthol cigarettes	박하 담배	pak·ha tam·bae
I'll take two packets.	두 갑 주세요.	tu kap chu·se·yo
I'd like a carton.	한 보루 주세요.	han po·ru chu·se·yo

filter-tipped	필터가 달린	p'il·t'ŏ·ga tal·lin
without filter	필터가 없는	p'il·t'ŏ·ga ŏm·nŭn

While we're on the subject of cigarettes, suppose you want to offer somebody one?

Would you like a cigarette?	담배 한 대 피우시겠어요?	tam·bae han·dae p'i·u·shi·ge·ssŏ·yo
Have one of mine.	제 것을 피우세요.	che·gŏ·sŭl p'i·u·se·yo
Try one of these.	이걸 피워 보시지요.	i·gŏl p'i·wŏ po·shi·ji·yo
They're very mild.	아주 순합니다.	a·ju sun·ham·ni·da
They're a bit strong.	좀 독하군요.	chom tok·ha·gun·yo

And if somebody offers you one?

Thank you.	고맙습니다.	ko·map·sŭm·ni·da
No, thanks.	아뇨, 괜찮습니다.	a·nyo kwen·ch'an·sŭm·ni·da
I don't smoke.	담배 피우지 않습니다.	tam·bae p'i·u·ji an·sŭm·ni·da
I've given up.	끊었읍니다.	kŭ·nŏ·ssŭm·ni·da

Your money: banks — currency

Money and traveller's cheques can be exchanged only at authorized currency exchanges, such as leading Western-style hotels, banks and top shops catering to foreign visitors. At larger places there is sure to be someone who speaks English. Remember to take your passport with you, as you may need it.

Hours

Banks are open from 9.30 a.m. to 4.30 p.m. on weekdays, and from 9.30 a.m. to 1.30 p.m. on Saturdays. All banks are closed on Sundays, but Kimp'o Airport's bank is open from 6.30 a.m. to 7.30 p.m. all the year round.

Monetary unit

The Korean monetary system is based on the *won*. The word *won* is abbreviated as ₩.

Value	Coin/note
1 won	aluminium coin
10 won	brass coin
50 won	nickel coin
100 won	nickel coin
500 won	banknote or nickel coin
1,000 won	banknote
5,000 won	banknote
10,000 won	banknote

Before going

Where's the nearest bank?	제일 가까운 은행이 어딥니까?	che·il ka·ka·un ŭn·haeng·i ŏ·dim·ni·ka
Where can I cash a traveller's cheque (check)?	여행자수표를 어디서 현금으로 바꿀 수 있읍니까?	yŏ·haeng·ja su·p'yo·rŭl ŏ·di·sŏ hyŏn·gŭm·ŭ·ro pa·kul·su i·ssŭm·ni·ka

Inside

I want to change some dollars.	달러를 바꾸고 싶은데요.	dal·lŏ·rŭl pa·ku·go shi·p'ŭn·de·yo
I'd like to change some pounds.	파운드를 바꾸고자 하는데요.	p'a·un·dŭ·rŭl pa·ku·go·ja ha·nŭn·de·yo
Here's my passport.	이것이 나의 여권입니다.	i·gŏ·shi na·ŭi yŏ·kwŏn·im·ni·da
What's the exchange rate?	환율은 얼맙니까?	hwan·yul·ŭn ŏl·mam·ni·ka
What rate of commission do you charge?	코미션은 얼마입니까?	k'o·mi·shŏn·ŭn ŏl·ma·im·ni·ka
Can you cash a personal cheque?	개인수표를 현금으로 바꿀 수 있읍니까?	kae·in su·p'yo·rŭl hyŏn·gŭm·ŭ·ro pa·kul·su i·ssŭm·ni·ka
How long will it take to clear the cheque?	수표를 교환 청산하는 데 시간이 얼마나 걸립니까?	su·p'yo·rŭl kyo·hwan ch'ŏng·san·ha·nŭn·de shi·gan·i ŏl·ma·na kŏl·lim·ni·ka
Can you cable my bank in ...?	...에 있는 나의 은행에 전보를 쳐줄 수 있읍니까?	...e in·nŭn na·ŭi ŭn·haeng·e chŏn·bo·rŭl ch'yŏ·jul·su i·ssŭm·ni·ka
I have ...	...이 있읍니다.	...i i·ssŭm·ni·da
a letter of credit	신용장	shin·yong·jang
an introduction from ...	...의 소개장	...ŭi so·gae·jang
a credit card	크레딧 카드	k'ŭ·re·dit k'a·dŭ
I'm expecting some money from the U.S. Has it arrived yet?	미국에서 돈이 오기로 되어있는데, 도착했읍니까?	mi·guk·e·sŏ ton·i o·gi·ro toe·ŏ·in·nŭn·de to·ch'ak·hae·ssŭm·ni·ka

Depositing

I want to credit this to my account.	이것을 나의 구좌에 넣어 주세요.	i·gŏ·sŭl na·ŭi ku·jwa·e nŏ·ŏ chu·se·yo
I want to credit this to Mr. Simon's account.	이 금액을 시몬씨의 구좌에 넣고 싶은데요.	i kŭ·mae·gŭl shi·mon·ssi·ŭi ku·jwa·e nŏ·k'o shi·p'ŭn·de·yo
Where should I sign?	어디에 사인을 할까요?	ŏ·di·e sa·in·ŭl hal·ka·yo

Currency converter

In a world of fluctuating currencies, we can offer no more than this do-it-yourself chart. You can get a card showing current exchange rates from banks, travel agencies and tourist offices. Why not fill in this chart, too, for handy reference?

Won	£	$
10		
50		
100		
500		
1,000		
5,000		
10,000		
50,000		
100,000		
500,000		
1,000,000		
5,000,000		

FOR NUMBERS, see page 175

Post Office

Post offices are indicated by a red and white ✹ sign. Mail boxes are painted red. Business hours are from 9 a.m. to 5 p.m. without a break.

Where's the nearest post office?	제일 가까운 우체국이 어 딥니까?	che·il ka·ka·un u·ch'e·gu·gi ŏ·dim·ni·ka
What time does the post office open?	우체국은 몇 시에 문을 엽니까?	u·ch'e·gu·gŭn myŏt·shi·e mun·ŭl yŏm·ni·ka
When does the post office close?	우체국은 몇 시에 문을 닫습니까?	u·ch'e·gu·gŭn myŏt·shi·e mun·ŭl ta·ssŭm·ni·ka
What window should I go to for stamps?	우표는 어느 창구에서 팝 니까?	u·p'yo·nŭn ŏ·nŭ ch'ang·gu·e·sŏ p'am·ni·ka
At which counter can I cash an international money order?	외국환은 어느 카운터입 니까?	oe·guk·hwan·ŭn ŏ·nŭ k'a·un·t'ŏ·im·ni·ka
I want . . . 50-won stamps and . . . 100-won stamps.	50 원짜리 우표 ···장과 100 원짜리 우표 ···장 주 세요.	o·ship·wŏn·cha·ri u·p'yo ... chang·gwa paek·wŏn·cha·ri u·p'yo ...chang chu·se·yo
What's the postage for a letter to the U.S.?	미국에 보내는 편지의 우 편요금은 얼맘니까?	mi·guk·e po·nae·nŭn p'yŏn·ji·ŭi u·p'yŏn·yo·gŭm·ŭn ŏl·mam·ni·ka
What's the postage for a postcard to Britain?	영국에 보내는 엽서의 우 편요금은 얼맘니까?	yŏng·guk·e po·nae·nŭn yŏp·sŏ·ŭi u·p'yŏn·yo·gŭm·ŭn ŏl·mam·ni·ka
When will this letter get there?	이 편지는 언제 도착할까 요?	i p'yŏn·ji·nŭn ŏn·je to·ch'ak·hal·ka·yo
Do all letters go airmail?	편지는 모두 항공편으로 갑니까?	p'yŏn·ji·nŭn mo·du hang·gong·p'yŏn·ŭ·ro kam·ni·ka
I want to send this parcel.	이 소포를 부치고 싶은데 요.	i so·p'o·rŭl pu·ch'i·go shi·p'ŭn·de·yo
Do I need to fill in a customs declaration form?	세관 신고용지에 기입해 야 합니까?	se·gwan shin·go·yong·ji·e ki·ip·hae·ya ham·ni·ka
I want to register this letter.	이 편지를 등기로 부치고 싶은데요.	i p'yŏn·ji·rŭl tŭng·gi·ro pu·ch'i·go shi·p'ŭn·de·yo

Where's the letter-box?	우체통은 어디에 있읍니까?	u·ch'e·t'ong·ŭn ŏ·di·e i·ssŭm·ni·ka
I want to send this (by) ...	이것을 …으로 부치고 싶은데요.	i·gŏ·sŭl ... ŭ·ro pu·ch'i·go shi·p'ŭn·de·yo
airmail	항공우편	hang·gong·u·p'yŏn
express (special delivery)	속달	sok·tal
recorded delivery	배달 증명	pae·dal chŭng·myŏng
registered mail	등기	tŭng·gi
Where's the poste restante (general delivery)?	유치 우편 창구는 어딥니까?	yu·ch'i u·p'yŏn ch'ang·gu·nŭn ŏ·dim·ni·ka
Is there any mail for me? My name is...	저에게 온 우편물이 있읍니까? 저의 이름은 …입니다.	chŏ·e·ge on u·p'yŏn·mu·ri i·ssŭm·ni·ka? chŏ·ŭi i·rŭm·ŭn ...im·ni·da
Here's my passport.	이것이 저의 여권입니다.	i·gŏ·shi chŏ·ŭi yŏ·kwŏn·im·ni·da

우표	STAMPS
소포	PARCELS
환	MONEY ORDERS

Cables (telegrams)

Where's the nearest cable office?	가장 가까운 전신국이 어딥니까?	ka·jang ka·ka·un chŏn·shin·gu·gi ŏ·dim·ni·ka
I want to send a cable (telegram). May I have a form, please?	전보를 치려고 하는데요. 용지를 주시겠어요?	chŏn·bo·rŭl ch'i·ryŏ·go ha·nŭn·de·yo yong·ji·rŭl chu·shi·ge·ssŏ·yo
How much is it per word?	한 자에 얼맙니까?	han cha·e ŏl·mam·ni·ka
How long will a cable to Boston take?	보스턴까지 전보로 시간이 얼마나 걸립니까?	bo·sŭ·t'ŏn·ka·ji chŏn·bo·ro shi·gan·i ŏl·ma·na kŏl·lim·ni·ka
Send it collect.	요금 수취인 부담으로 치세요.	yo·gŭm su·ch'wi·in pu·dam·ŭro ch'i·se·yo

Telephoning

There are many public telephone booths in the streets. If you can't find one, however, you can always try a tea-room, a bar or a railway station. For domestic calls, direct dialling is used in most cities. There are two kinds of public telephone, identifiable by colour and size: the red phones are for local calls; the grey ones are reserved for intercity calls.

To continue a call keep inserting a coin every time you hear the warning chime. Excess coins will be returned when you have finished. For overseas calls, a card phone can be used for International Subscriber Dialling (ISD). Between the hours of 9 p.m. and 8 a.m. international telephone rates are reduced.

General

Where's the telephone?	전화는 어디에 있읍니까?	chŏn·hwa·nŭn ŏ·di·e i·ssŭm·ni·ka
Where's the nearest telephone booth?	가장 가까운 공중 전화는 어딥니까?	ka·jang ka·ka·un kong·jung chŏn·hwa·nŭn ŏ·dim·ni·ka
May I use your phone?	전화 좀 써도 됩니까?	chŏn·hwa chom ssŏ·do toem·ni·ka
Have you a telephone directory for Seoul?	서울의 전화번호부가 있읍니까?	sŏ·ul·ŭi chŏn·hwa pŏn·ho·bu·ga i·ssŭm·ni·ka
Can you help me get this number?	이 번호에 좀 걸어 주시겠읍니까?	i pŏn·ho·e chom kŏ·rŏ chu·shi·ge·ssŭm·ni·ka

Operator

Do you speak English?	영어를 하십니까?	yŏng·ŏ·rŭl ha·shim·ni·ka
Good morning. I want Seoul 123-4567.	안녕하세요. 서울 123-4567 번을 부탁합니다.	an·nyŏng·ha·se·yo sŏ·ul 123-4567 pŏn· ŭl pu·t'ak· ham·ni·da
Can I dial direct?	DDD가 됩니까?	di·di·di·ga toem·ni·ka

FOR NUMBERS, see page 175

I want to place a person-to-person call.	특정인 호출 전화를 부탁합니다.	t'ŭk·chŏng·in ho·ch'ul chŏn·hwa·rŭl pu·t'ak·ham·ni·da
I want to reverse the charges (call collect).	콜렉트 콜로 부탁합니다.	k'ol·lek·t'ŭ k'ol·lo pu·t'ak·ham·ni·da
Will you tell me the cost of the call afterwards?	요금은 나중에 알려 주시겠어요?	yo·gŭm·ŭn na·jung·e al·lyŏ chu·shi·ge·ssŏ·yo

Speaking

I want to speak to ...	…과 통화하고 싶은데요.	... kwa t'ong·hwa·ha·go shi·p'ŭn·de·yo
Would you put me through to ...?	…을 부탁합니다.	...ŭl pu·t'ak·ham·ni·da
I want extension ...	구내 …을 부탁합니다.	ku·nae ...ŭl pu·t'ak·ham·ni·da
Is that ...?	거기 …입니까?	kŏ·gi ... im·ni·ka
Hello. This is ...	여보세요. 여기는 …입니다.	yŏ·bo·se·yo yŏ·gi·nŭn ...im·ni·da

Bad luck

| Would you try again later, please? | 나중에 다시 한번 걸어 주시겠어요? | na·jung·e ta·shi han·bŏn kŏ·rŏ chu·shi·ge·ssŏ·yo |
| Operator, you gave me the wrong number. | 교환, 다른 번호였어요. | kyo·hwan ta·rŭn pŏn·ho·yŏ·ssŏ·yo |

Not there

| When will he/she be back? | 언제 돌아오실까요? | ŏn·je to·ra·o·shil·ka·yo |
| Will you tell him/her I called? My name is ... | 전화 왔다고 전해 주시겠어요? 저는 …이라고 합니다. | chŏn·hwa wa·ssŏ·ta·go chŏn·hae chu·shi·ge·ssŏ·yo? chŏ·nŭn ...i·ra·go·ham·ni·da |

FOR NUMBERS, see p. 179

| Would you ask him/her to call me? | 저에게 전화하라고 전해 주시겠어요? | chŏ·e·ge chŏn·hwa·ha·ra·go chŏn·hae chu·shi·ge·ssŏ·yo |
| Would you take a message, please? | 말씀 좀 전해 주시겠어요? | mal·ssŭm chom chŏn·hae chu·shi·ge·ssŏ·yo |

Charges

| What was the cost of that call? | 그 전화 요금은 얼마나 나왔읍니까? | kŭ chŏn·hwa yo·gŭm·ŭn ŏl·ma·na na·wa·ssŭm·ni·ka |
| I want to pay for the call. | 전화 요금을 지불하려고 하는데요. | chŏn·hwa yo·gŭm·ŭl chi·bul·ha·ryŏ·go ha·nŭn·de·yo |

You may hear...

전화 왔읍니다.	There's a telephone call for you.
전화 왔읍니다.	You're wanted on the telephone.
몇번에 거셨읍니까?	What number are you calling?
통화중입니다.	The line's engaged.
대답이 없는데요.	There's no answer.
잘못 거셨읍니다.	You've got the wrong number.
전화가 고장입니다.	The phone is out of order.
그는 지금 외출중입니다.	He's out at the moment.

The Car

We'll begin this section by considering your possible needs at a filling station. Most filling stations don't handle major repairs; but apart from selling fuel, they may be helpful in solving all kinds of minor problems.

Where's the nearest filling (service) station?	제일 가까운 주유소가 어 딥니까?	che·il ka·ka·un chu·yu·so· ga ŏ·dim·ni·ka
I want ... litres, please.	···리터 넣어 주세요.	... ri·t'ŏ nŏ·ŏ chu·se·yo
I want 15 litres of standard.	스탠더드를 15리터 넣어 주세요.	sŭ·t'aen·dŏ·dŭ·rŭl 15 ri·t'ŏ nŏ·ŏ chu·se·yo
I want 25 litres of super.	수퍼를 25리터 넣어 주 세요.	su·p'ŏ·rŭl 25 ri·t'ŏ nŏ·ŏ chu·se·yo
Give me 2,000 won worth of...	···을 2,000원어치 넣어 주세요.	... ŭl 2,000 wŏn·ŏ·ch'i nŏ·ŏ chu·se·yo
Fill it up, please.	가득히 넣어 주세요.	ka·dŭk·hi nŏ·ŏ chu·se·yo
Check the oil and water, please.	오일과 물을 좀 봐주세 요.	o·il·gwa mul·ŭl chom pwa· ju·se·yo
Give me ... litres of oil.	오일을 ···리터 주세요.	o·il·ŭl ... ri·t'ŏ chu·se·yo
Top(fill) up the battery with distilled water.	밧데리의 물을 넣어 주 세요.	ba·t'e·ri·ŭi mul·ŭl nŏ·ŏ chu·se·yo
Check the brake fluid.	브레이크 오일을 봐주세 요.	bŭ·re·i·k'ŭ o·il·ŭl pwa· ju·se· yo

Fluid measures					
litres	imp. gal.	U.S. gal.	litres	imp. gal.	U.S. gal.
5	1.1	1.3	30	6.6	7.8
10	2.2	2.6	35	7.7	9.1
15	3.3	3.9	40	8.8	10.4
20	4.4	5.2	45	9.9	11.7
25	5.5	6.5	50	11.0	13.0

FOR NUMBERS, see page 175

Tyre pressure			
lb./sq. in.	kg/cm²	lb./sq. in.	kg/cm²
10	0.7	26	1.8
12	0.8	27	1.9
15	1.1	28	2.0
18	1.3	30	2.1
20	1.4	33	2.3
21	1.5	36	2.5
23	1.6	38	2.7
24	1.7	40	2.8

Would you check the tires?	타이어를 좀 봐주시겠어요?	t'a·i·ŏ·rŭl chom pwa·ju·shi·ge·ssŏ·yo
The pressure should be 1.6 front, 1.8 rear.	압력은 앞이 1.6, 뒤가 1.8이어야 합니다.	am·nyŏk·ŭn a·p'i 1.6 twi·ga 1.8·i·ŏ·ya ham·ni·da
Check the spare tyre too, please.	스페어 타이어도 좀 봐주세요.	sŭ·p'e·ŏ t'a·i·ŏ·do chom pwa·ju·se·yo
Can you mend this puncture(fix this flat)?	펑크를 수리해 주시겠어요?	p'ŏng·k'ŭ·rŭl su·ri·hae chu·shi·ge·ssŏ·yo
Would you change this tyre, please?	이 타이어를 갈아 주시겠어요?	i t'a·i·ŏ·rŭl ka·ra chu·shi·ge·ssŏ·yo
Would you clean the windscreen (windshield)?	앞 유리를 닦아 주시겠어요?	am·nyu·ri·rŭl ta·ka chu·shi·ge·ssŏ·yo
Have you a road map of this district?	이 지방의 도로 지도를 갖고 계십니까?	i chi·bang·ŭi to·ro chi·do·rŭl ka·ko kye·shim·ni·ka
Where are the toilets?	화장실이 어딥니까?	hwa·jang·shil·i ŏ·dim·ni·ka

CAR—FILLING STATION

Asking the way—Street directions

Excuse me.	실례합니다.	shil·lye·ham·ni·da
Can you tell me the way to ...?	...으로 가는 길을 가르쳐 주시겠어요?	... ŭ·ro ka·nŭn kil·ŭl ka·rŭ·ch'yŏ chu·shi·ge·ssŏ·yo
How do I get to ...?	...에는 어떻게 가면 됩니까?	... e·nŭn ŏ·tŏ·ke ka·myŏn toem·ni·ka

Where does this road lead to?	이 길은 어디로 가는 길입니까?	i kil·ŭn ŏ·di·ro ka·nŭn kil·im·ni·ka
Can you show me on this map where I am?	이 지도에서 내가 있는 곳을 가리켜 주시겠읍니까?	i chi·do·e·sŏ nae·ga in·nŭn ko·sŭl ka·ri·k'yŏ chu·shi·ge·ssŭm·ni·ka
How far is it to ... from here?	여기서 …까지는 거리가 얼마나 됩니까?	yŏ·gi·sŏ ... ka·ji·nŭn kŏ·ri·ga ŏl·ma·na toem·ni·ka

Miles into kilometres										
1 mile = 1.609 kilometres (km)										
miles	10	20	30	40	50	60	70	80	90	100
km	16	32	48	64	80	97	113	129	145	161

Kilometres into miles													
1 kilometre (km) = 0.62 miles													
km	10	20	30	40	50	60	70	80	90	100	110	120	130
miles	6	12	19	25	31	37	44	50	56	62	68	75	81

Possible answers

길을 잘못 드셨읍니다.	You're on the wrong road.
곧장 가십시오.	Go straight ahead.
이 길을 가다가 왼쪽(오른쪽)입니다.	It's down there on the left (right).
저쪽으로 가십시오.	Go that way.
첫번째(두번째) 네거리까지 가십시오.	Go to the first (second) cross-road.
신호등이 있는 데서 왼쪽(오른쪽)으로 도십시오.	Turn left (right) at the traffic lights.

In the rest of this section, we'll be more closely concerned with the car itself. We've divided it into two parts:

Part A contains general advice on motoring in Korea. It's essentially for reference and, therefore, to be browsed over, preferably in advance.

Part B is concerned with the practical details of accidents and breakdown. It includes a list of car parts and a list of things that may go wrong with them. All you have to do is to show the lists to the garage mechanic and get him to point to the items required.

Part A

Customs—Documentation

Bringing private cars into Korea isn't as simple as in other countries and involves a considerable amount of red tape. You are therefore advised to ask the Korean embassy or consulate in your country for full details.

You'll also require the following documents:
    passport
    international insurance certificate (green card)
    international driving licence

The nationality plate or sticker must be on the car. A red triangle—for display on the road in case of accidents—is a very important accessory, and parking lights are advisable.

Here's my ...	이것이 저의 …입니다.	i·gŏ·shi chŏ·ŭi . . . im·ni·da
driving licence	운전 면허증	un·jŏn myŏn·hŏ·jŭng
green card	보험 증서	po·hŏm·jŭng·sŏ
passport	여권	yŏ·gwŏn
I have nothing to declare.	아무것도 신고할 것이 없읍니다.	a·mu·gŏt·do shin·go·hal kŏ·shi ŏp·sŭm·ni·da
I have ...	…을 갖고 있읍니다.	. . . ŭl kat·ko i·ssŭm·ni·da
a carton of cigarettes	담배 한 보루	tam·bae han po·ru
a bottle of whisky	위스키 한 병	wi·sŭ·k'i han pyŏng
a bottle of wine	포도주 한 병	p'o·do·ju han pyŏng
We're staying for ...	…간 체재할 생각입니다.	. . . gan ch'e·jae·hal saeng·gak·im·ni·da
a week	1 주일	il·chu·il
two weeks	2 주일	i·ju·il
a month	1 개월	il·gae·wŏl

Roads

The road classification and map references in Korea are as follows:

ko·sok·to·ro (motorway/expressway), a toll is charged according to the distance to be travelled and the size of the car.

kuk·to—first-class main road.

Excellent bilingual road maps can be obtained from travel agencies.

In Korea, as in America, all driving is done on the right. Driving around in Korea on your own, however, except possibly on newly-built super-highways, should be done with the utmost caution, particularly on crowded city streets where drivers often disregard traffic safety rules. Use of taxis, buses and limousine service is, therefore, highly recommended whenever and wherever possible.

International road signs are used throughout Korea though you'll find a list of special Korean-language signs on page 148.

Pedestrians should pay great attention at the striped crossings which — theoretically — allow them to cross the road in safety: Korean drivers are not always as disciplined as they might be.

Parking

Use your common sense when parking. The police are normally lenient with foreign tourists, but don't push your luck too far. Obey the parking regulations indicated by signs or white lines painted on the kerb (curb).

Excuse me. May I park here?	실례합니다. 여기에 주차해도 됩니까?	shil·lye·ham·ni·da yŏ·gi·e chu·ch'a·hae·do toem·ni·ka
How long may I park here?	여기에 얼마나 주차할 수 있읍니까?	yŏ·gi·e ŏl·ma·na chu·ch'a·hal su i·ssŭm·ni·ka
What's the charge for parking here?	여기에 주차하는 데 요금이 얼마입니까?	yŏ·gi·e chu·ch'a·ha·nŭn·de yo·gŭm·i ŏl·ma·im·ni·ka
Must I leave my lights on?	라이트를 켜두지 않으면 안됩니까?	ra·i·t'ŭ·rŭl k'yŏ·du·ji an·ŭ·myŏn an·doem·ni·ka

Korean road signs

Here are some of the main signs and notices you are likely to encounter when driving in Korea:

감속운행	Reduce speed
건널목 있음	Level (railroad) crossing
노면불량	Bad road surface
높이 제한	Height limit
도로 공사중	Roadworks in progress
막혔음	Cul-de-sac (dead-end road)
버스 정류장	Bus stop
보행자 전용	Pedestrians only
보행자 주의	Caution : pedestrians
본선	Through traffic
서행	Slow
안전운행	Drive safely
우선	Priority (right of way)
우회로	Diversion (detour)
위험	danger
위험 커브	Dangerous bend (curve)
이 방향 교통	Oncoming traffic
일방 통행	One-way traffic
자갈길	Loose gravel
자전거 전용	Bicycles only
전방에 간선도로 있음	Main road (thoroughfare) ahead
전방에 신호등 있음	Traffic lights ahead
정지	Stop
좌회전 가능	Left turn allowed at any time
주의	Caution
주정차 금지	No parking or stopping
주차 금지	No parking
중량 제한	Weight limit
차량 통행금지	No vehicles
추월 금지	No overtaking (passing)
회전 금지	No U turn
횡단 보도	Pedestrian crossing

FOR ROAD SIGNS, see also pages 160 and 161

Part B

Accidents

This section is confined to immediate aid. The legal problems of responsibility and settlement can be taken care of at a later stage. Your first concern will be for the injured.

Is anyone hurt?	부상자가 있읍니까?	pu·sang·ja·ga i·ssŭm·ni·ka
Don't move.	움직이지 마세요.	um·ji·gi·ji ma·se·yo
It's all right. Don't worry.	괜찮아요. 염려마세요.	kwen·ch'an·a·yo yŏm·nyŏ ma·se·yo
Where's the nearest telephone?	전화가 있는 제일 가까운 데가 어딥니까?	chŏn·hwa·ga in·nŭn che·il ka·ka·un te·ga ŏ·dim·ni·ka
May I use your telephone?	전화 좀 써도··됩니까?	chŏn·hwa chom ssŏ·do toem·ni·ka
There's been an accident.	사고가 났어요.	sa·go·ga na·ssŏ·yo
Call a doctor (ambulance) quickly.	빨리 의사(구급차)를 불러 주세요.	pal·li ŭi·sa (ku·gŭp·ch'a)· rŭl pul·lŏ chu·se·yo
There are people injured.	부상자가 있읍니다.	pu·sang·ja·ga i·ssŭm·ni·da
Help me get them out of the car.	차에서 들어내도록 좀도 와 주세요.	ch'a·e·sŏ tŭ·rŏ·nae·do·rok chom to·wa chu·se·yo

Police—Exchange of information

Please call the police.	경찰을 불러 주세요.	kyŏng·ch'al·ŭl pul·lŏ chu·se·yo
There's been an accident.	사고가 났어요.	sa·go·ga na·ssŏ·yo
It's about 2km from ...	현장은 …에서 2킬로쯤 떨어진 곳입니다.	hyŏn·jang·ŭn ... e·sŏ 2 k'il· lo·chŭm tŏ·rŏ·jin ko·shim· ni·da
I'm on the Seoul-Pusan road, 13km from Seoul.	경부 고속도로에 있읍니 다. 서울에서 13킬로 지점입니다.	kyŏng·bu ko·sok·to·ro·e i·ssŭm·ni·da sŏ·ul·e·sŏ 13 k'il·lo chi·jŏm·im·ni·da

Here's my name and address.	이것이 저의 이름과 주소 입니다.	i·gŏ·shi chŏ·ŭi i·rŭm·gwa chu·so·im·ni·da
Would you mind acting as a witness?	증인이 되어 주시지 않 겠읍니까 ?	chŭng·in·i toe·ŏ chu·shi·ji an·k'e·ssŭm·ni·ka
I'd like an interpreter.	통역이 있었으면 좋겠는 데요.	t'ong·yŏ·gi i·ssŏ·ssŭ·myŏn cho·k'en·nŭn·de·yo

Remember to put out a red warning triangle if the car is out of action or impeding traffic flow.

Breakdown

... and that's what we'll do with this section: break it down into four phases.

1. **On the road**
   You ask where the nearest garage is.
2. **At the garage**
   You tell the mechanic what's wrong.
3. **Finding the trouble**
   He tells you what he thinks is wrong.
4. **Getting it fixed**
   You tell him to fix it and, once that is done, settle the account (or argue about it).

Phase 1—On the road

| Where's the nearest garage? | 제일 가까운 수리소가 어딥니까 ? | che·il ka·ka·un su·ri·so·ga ŏ·dim·ni·ka |
| Excuse me. My car has broken down. May I use your phone? | 죄송합니다. 차가 고장 나서 그러는데요, 전화 좀 쓸 수 없을까요 ? | choe·song·ham·ni·da. ch'a·ga ko·jang·na·sŏ kŭ·rŏ·nŭn·de·yo chŏn·hwa chom ssŭl·su ŏp·sŭl·ka·yo |

What's the telephone number of the nearest garage?	가장 가까운 수리소의 전화번호가 몇번입니까?	ka·jang ka·ka·un su·ri·so·ŭi chŏn·hwa pŏn·ho·ga myŏt· bŏn·im·ni·ka
I've had a breakdown at ...	…에서 차가 고장났는데요.	... e·sŏ ch'a·ga ko·jang· nan·nŭn·de·yo
We're on the Seoul–Pusan motorway (expressway), about 13km from Seoul.	서울 부산간 고속도로의, 서울에서 13킬로 지점에 있읍니다.	sŏ·ul pu·san·gan ko·sok· to·ro·ŭi sŏ·ul·e·sŏ 13 k'il·lo chi·jŏm·e i·ssŭm·ni·da
Can you send a mechanic?	정비공을 보내 주시겠읍니까?	chŏng·bi·gong·ŭl po·nae chu·shi·ge·ssŭm·ni·ka
Can you send a van (truck) to tow my car?	레카차를 보내 주실 수 있읍니까?	re·k'a·ch'a·rŭl po·nae chu· shil su i·ssŭm·ni·ka
How long will you be?	오시는 데 시간이 얼마나 걸리겠읍니까?	o·shi·nŭn·de shi·gan·i ŏl· ma·na kŏl·li·ge·ssŭm·ni·ka

Phase 2—At the garage

Can you help me?	부탁 좀 들어주시겠읍니까?	pu·t'ăk chom tŭ·rŏ·ju· shi·ge·ssŭm·ni·ka
Can you repair my car?	제 차를 수리해 주실 수 있을까요?	che ch'a·rŭl su·ri·hae chu· shil·su i·ssŭl·ka·yo
I don't know what's wrong with it.	어디가 잘못됐는지 모르겠어요.	ŏ·di·ga chal·mot·dwen·nŭn·ji mo·rŭ·ge·ssŏ·yo
I think there's something wrong with the ...	…이 잘못된 것 같은데요.	... i chal·mot·doen kŏt ka· t'ŭn·de·yo
battery	밧데리	ba·t'e·ri
brakes	브레이크	bŭ·re·i·k'ŭ
bulbs	라이트	ra·i·t'ŭ
clutch	클러치	k'ŭl·lŏ·ch'i
cooling system	냉각장치	naeng·gak chang·ch'i
contact	접촉 부분	chŏp·ch'ok pu·bun
dimmers	광도 낮추는 장치	kwang·do na·ch'u·nŭn chang·ch'i
dynamo	발전기	pal·chŏn·gi

electrical system	전기 장치	chŏn·gi chang·ch'i
engine	엔진	en·jin
gears	기어	ki·ŏ
generator	발전기	pal·jŏn·gi
handbrake	핸드브레이크	haen·dŭ·bŭ·re·i·k'ŭ
headlight	헤드라이트	he·dŭ·ra·i·t'ŭ
horn	경적	kyŏng·jŏk
ignition system	점화 장치	chŏm·hwa chang·ch'i
indicator	방향 지시기	pang·hyang chi·shi·gi
lights	라이트	ra·i·t'ŭ
brake light	브레이크 등	bŭ·re·i·k'ŭ tŭng
reversing (backup) light	후진등	hu·jin·dŭng
tail lights	후미등	hu·mi·dŭng
lubrication system	윤활유 장치	yun·hwal·yu chang·ch'i
pedal	페달	p'e·dal
reflectors	반사경	pan·sa·gyŏng
spark (ing) plugs	점화 플러그	chŏm·hwa p'ŭl·lŏ·gŭ
starting motor	스타터	sŭ·t'a·t'ŏ
steering	핸들	haen·dŭl
suspension	차대받이 장치	ch'a·dae·ba·ji chang·ch'i
transmission	전동 장치	chŏn·dong chang·ch'i
wheels	바퀴	pa·k'wi
wipers	와이퍼	wa·i·p'ŏ

RIGHT	LEFT		FRONT	BACK
오른쪽	왼쪽		앞	뒤
(o·rŭn·chok)	(oen·chok)		(ap)	(twi)

It's...	...	...
bad	나쁩니다.	na·pŭm·ni·da
blowing	샙니다.	saem·ni·da
blown	용해되고 있습니다.	yong·hae·doe·go i·ssŭm·ni·da
broken	고장났습니다.	ko·jang·na·ssŭm·ni·da
burnt	탔습니다.	t'a·ssŭm·ni·da
cracked	금이 갔습니다.	kŭ·mi ka·ssŭm·ni·da
defective	불량합니다.	pul·lyang·ham·ni·da
disconnected	벗겨졌습니다.	pŏt·kyŏ·jŏ·ssŭm·ni·da
dry	말랐습니다.	mal·la·ssŭm·ni·da
frozen	얼었습니다.	ŏ·rŏ·ssŭm·ni·da

jammed	움직이지 않습니다.	um·ji·gi·ji an·sŭm·ni·da
knocking	노킹 소리를 내고 있읍니다.	no·k'ing so·ri·rŭl nae·go i·ssŭm·ni·da
leaking	샙니다.	saem·ni·da
loose	느슨합니다.	nŭ·sŭn·ham·ni·da
misfiring	점화되지 않습니다.	chŏm·hwa·doe·ji an·sŭm·ni·da
noisy	소리가 납니다.	so·ri·ga nam·ni·da
not working	움직이지 않습니다.	um·ji·gi·ji an·sŭm·ni·da
overheating	과열되었읍니다.	kwa·yŏl·doe·ŏ·ssŭm·ni·da
short-circuiting	누전입니다.	nu·jŏn·im·ni·da
slack	헐렁합니다.	hŏl·lŏng·ham·ni·da
slipping	미끄러집니다.	mi·kŭ·rŏ·jim·ni·da
stuck	붙었읍니다.	pu·t'ŏ·ssŭm·ni·da
vibrating	진동합니다.	chin·dong·ham·ni·da
weak	약합니다.	yak·ham·ni·da
worn	닳았읍니다.	ta·ra·ssŭm·ni·da
The car won't start.	시동이 걸리지 않습니다.	shi·dong·i kŏl·li·ji an·sŭm·ni·da
It's locked and the keys are inside.	열쇠를 안에 둔 채 잠궈 버렸읍니다.	yŏl·soe·rŭl an·e tun·ch'ae cham·gwŏ·bŏ·ryŏ·ssŭm·ni·da
The fan-belt is too slack.	팬 벨트가 너무 느슨합니다.	p'aen·bel·t'ŭ·ga nŏ·mu nŭ·sŭn·ham·ni·da
The radiator is leaking.	라지에타가 샙니다.	ra·ji·e·t'a·ga saem·ni·da
The idling needs adjusting.	캬브레타의 아이들링을 조절해야 되겠어요.	k'ya·bŭ·re·t'a·ŭi a·i·dŭl·ling·ŭl cho·jŏl·hae·ya toe·ge·ssŏ·yo
The clutch engages too quickly.	클러치 유격이 너무 적어요.	k'ŭl·lŏ·ch'i yu·gyŏ·gi nŏ·mu chŏ·gŏ·yo
The steering wheel is vibrating.	핸들이 떨립니다.	haen·dŭ·ri tŏl·lim·ni·da
The wipers are smearing.	와이퍼가 더러워졌읍니다.	wa·i·p'ŏ·ga tŏ·rŏ·wŏ·jyŏ·ssŭm·ni·da
The pedal needs adjusting.	페달을 조절해야겠어요.	p'e·da·rŭl cho·jŏl·hae·ya·ge·ssŏ·yo

Now that you've explained what's wrong, you'll want to know how long it'll take to repair it and organize yourself accordingly.

How long will it take to repair?	고치는 데 시간이 얼마나 걸립니까?	ko·ch'i·nŭn·de shi·gan·i ŏl·ma·na kŏl·lim·ni·ka
Shall I come back in half an hour (tomorrow)?	30분내에(내일) 올깨요.	sam·ship·pun·nae·e (nae·il) ol·ke·yo
Can you give me a lift into town?	시내까지 태워다 주실 수 있어요?	shi·nae·ka·ji t'ae·wŏ·da chu·shil·su i·ssŏ·yo
Is there a place to stay nearby?	요근처에 숙박할 만한 데 가 있읍니까?	yo·gŭn·ch'ŏ·e suk·pak·hal·man·han te·ga i·ssŭm·ni·ka
May I use your phone?	전화 좀 써도 됩니까?	chŏn·hwa chom ssŏ·do toem·ni·ka

Phase 3—Finding the trouble

If you don't know what's wrong with the car, it's up to the mechanic to find the trouble. You can ask him what has to be repaired by handing him the book and pointing to the Korean text below.

다음 리스트를 보시고 고장난 데를 가리켜 주세요. 그리고, 고장 상태에 관해서는 다음 페이지의 리스트를 보아 주세요.*

공기 여과장치	air filter
공기 차대받이 장치	pneumatic suspension
그리스	grease
기어	gear
기어박스	gearbox
냉각장치	cooling system
라이닝	lining
라지에타	radiator
래크 앤드 피년	rack and pinion

*Please look at the following alphabetical list and point to the defective item. If your customer wants to know what is wrong with it, pick the applicable term from the next list (broken, short-circuited, etc.).

링	rings
막	diaphragm
메인 베어링	main bearings
물 펌프	water pump
바퀴	wheels
발전기	dynamo (generator)
밧데리	battery
밧데리 셀	battery cells
밧데리 액	battery liquid
배전기	distributor
배전기 도선	distributor leads
밸브	valve
밸브 스프링	valve spring
베어링	bearing
변속기	transmission
부구	float
브러시	brushes
브레이크	brake
브레이크 드럼	brake drum
스타터	starting motor
스티어링	steering
스티어링 박스	steering box
스템	stems
스프링	springs
실린더	cylinder
실린더 블럭	cylinder block
실린더 패킹	cylinder head gasket
실린더 헤드	cylinder head
안정장치	stabilizer
압력 스프링	pressure-springs
엔진	engine
연결부분	connection
오일 여과장치	oil filter
온도 조절장치	thermostat
완충기	shock-absorber
자동 변속기	automatic transmission
자재 이음쇠	universal joint
전기 장치	electrical system
점화 코일	ignition coil
점화 플러그	spark(ing) plugs
점화플러그 도선	spark(ing) plug leads
접촉점	contact
죠인트	joint

CAR—REPAIRS

주입펌프	injection pump
차대받이 장치	suspension
캠축	camshaft
캬브레타	carburettor
케이블	cable
크랭크 덮개	crankcase
크랭크 축	crankshaft
클러치	clutch
클러치 페달	clutch pedal
클러치 플레이트	clutch plate
타이어의 겉싸개	shoes
태핏	tappets
톱니	teeth
펌프	pump
포인트	points
피스톤	piston
피스톤 링	piston rings
필터	filter
핸들축	steering column
후앙	fan
후앙벨트	fan-belt
휘발유 여과장치	petrol filter
휘발유 펌프	petrol pump

다음 리스트에는 고장의 상태 및 수리법이 적혀 있읍니다. *

과열된	overheating
교체하다	to replace
교환하다	to change
균형을 잡다	to balance
금이 간	cracked
깨진, 고장난	broken
낮은	low
노킹소리가 나는	knocking
놀기	play
높은	high
누전된	short-circuit
느슨하게 하다	to loosen
느슨한	loose

* The following list contains words about what's wrong or what may have to be done with the car.

더럽혀진	dirty
라이닝을 갈다	to reline
마른	dry
마모된	worn
미끄러지는	slipping
벗겨진, 연결되지 않은	disconnected
부식된	corroded
분해하다	to strip down
불량한	defective
붙어버린	stuck
빠른	quick
새고 있는	blowing
새고 있는	leaking
약한	weak
얼어붙은	frozen
연마하다	to grind in
용해된	blown
움직이지 않는	jammed
점화하지 않는	misfiring
조절하다	to adjust
죄다	to tighten
진동하는	vibrating
짧은	short
청소하다	to clean
충전하다	to charge
탄, 연소된	burnt
펑크	puncture
헐렁한	slack
휜, 구부러진	warped

Phase 4—Getting it fixed

Have you found the trouble?	잘못된 데를 발견했읍니까?	chal·mot·doen de·rŭl pal·gyŏn·hae·ssŭm·ni·ka

Now that you know what's wrong, or at least have some idea, you may want to find out...

Is that serious?	심합니까?	shim·ham·ni·ka
Can you fix it?	고칠 수 있읍니까?	ko·ch'il·su i·ssŭm·ni·ka
Can you do it now?	지금 할 수 있읍니까?	chi·gŭm hal·su i·ssŭm·ni·ka
What's it going to cost?	비용은 얼마나 됩니까?	pi·yong·ŭn ŏl·ma·na toem·ni·ka
Have you the necessary spare parts?	필요한 부품이 있읍니까?	p'i·ryo·han pu·p'um·i i·ssŭm·ni·ka

What if he says "no"?

Why can't you do it?	왜 안됩니까?	we an·doem·ni·ka
Is it essential to have that part?	그 부품이 없으면 안됩니까?	kŭ pu·p'um·i ŏp·sŭ·myŏn an·doem·ni·ka
How long is it going to take to get the spare parts?	부품을 구입하는 데 시간이 얼마나 걸립니까?	pu·p'um·ŭl ku·ip·ha·nŭn·de shi·gan·i ŏl·ma·na kŏl·lim·ni·ka
Where's the nearest garage that can repair it?	그것을 수리할 수 있는 가장 가까운 수리소는 어디에 있읍니까?	kŭ·gŏ·sŭl su·ri·hal·su·in·nŭn ka·jang ka·ka·un su·ri·so·nŭn ŏ·di·e i·ssŭm·ni·ka
Well, can you fix it so that I can get as far as...?	그럼 …까지 갈 수 있게만 해주시겠어요?	kŭ·rŏm ... ka·ji kal·su it·ke·man hae·ju·shi·ge·ssŏ·yo

If you're really stuck, ask if you can leave the car at the garage.
Contact an automobile association ... or hire another car.

Settling the bill

| Is everything fixed? | 모두 수리가 되었읍니까? | mo·du su·ri·ga toe·ŏ·ssŭm·ni·ka |
| How much do I owe you? | 요금이 얼마입니까? | yo·gŭm·i ŏl·ma·im·ni·ka |

The garage then presents you with a bill. If you're satisfied . . .

Will you take a traveller's cheque(check)?	여행자 수표도 괜찮습니까?	yŏ·haeng·ja su·p'yo·do kwen·ch'an·sŭm·ni·ka
Thank you very much for your help.	도와주셔서 대단히 감사합니다.	to·wa·ju·syŏ·sŏ tae·dan·hi kam·sa·ham·ni·da
This is for you.	이것은 그냥 드리는 겁니다.	i·gŏ·sŭn kŭ·nyang tŭ·ri·nŭn kŏm·ni·da

But you may feel that the workmanship is sloppy or that you're paying for work not done. Get the bill itemized. If necessary, get it translated before you pay.

| I'd like to check the bill first. Will you itemize the work done? | 우선 청구서를 확인하고 싶은데요. 수리한 명세서를 주시겠어요? | u·sŏn ch'ŏng·gu·sŏ·rŭl hwa·gin·ha·go shi·p'ŭn·de·yo su·ri·han myŏng·se·sŏ·rŭl chu·shi·ge·ssŏ·yo |

If the garage still won't back down—and you're sure you're right—get the help of a third party.

Some Korean road signs

Road closed

No bicycles

No entry

No automobiles

No right turn

No U turn

No overtaking

No vehicles carrying explosive or inflammable materials

Minimum speed

Speed limit

No stopping

No parking

Stop

Slow down

Use of horn prohibited

Crossing by pedestrians prohibited

School
crossing

Straight and
right turn

Left turn

Roundabout

Automobiles
only

Sound horn

Go straight

Pedestrian
crossing

일방통행

One way

Road divides

Bicycle path

Pedestrian
path

Snow tyre
or chain

Keep
to the right

주차
PARKING

Parking

Safety zone

Doctor

Frankly, how much use is a phrase book going to be to you in the case of serious injury or illness? The only phrase you need in such an emergency is . . .

Get a doctor—quick!	의사를 불러 주세요—빨리!	ŭi·sa·rŭl pul·lŏ chu·se·yo—pal·li!

But there are minor aches and pains, ailments and irritations that can upset the best-planned trip. Here we can help you—and, perhaps, the doctor.

Some doctors will speak English well; others will know enough for your needs. But suppose there is something the doctor cannot explain because of language difficulties? We've thought of that.

As you will see, this section has been arranged to enable you and the doctor to communicate. From page 165 to 171, you will find your side of the dialogue on the upper half of each page; the doctor's is on the lower half.

The whole section has been divided into three parts: illness, wounds, nervous tension. Page 171 is concerned with prescriptions and fees.

General

I need a doctor —quickly.	의사를 불러 주세요. 빨리.	ŭi·sa·rŭl pul·lŏ chu·se·yo. pal·li
Can you get me a doctor?	의사를 불러 주시겠어요?	ŭi·sa·rŭl pul·lŏ chu·shi·ge·ssŏ·yo
Is there a doctor in the hotel?	호텔에 의사가 있읍니까?	ho·t'el·e ŭi·sa·ga i·ssŭm·ni·ka
Please telephone for a doctor immediately.	전화로 곧 의사를 불러 주세요.	chŏn·hwa·ro kot ŭi·sa·rŭl pul·lŏ chu·se·yo
Where's a doctor who speaks English?	영어를 할 줄 아는 의사는 어디 가면 있을까요?	yŏng·ŏ·rŭl hal·chul a·nŭn ŭi·sa·nŭn ŏ·di ka·myŏn i·ssŭl·ka·yo

DOCTOR

Is there an English/American hospital in town?	이 거리에 영국/미국 병원이 있읍니까?	i kŏ·ri·e yŏng·guk/mi·guk pyŏng·wŏn·i i·ssŭm·ni·ka
Where's the surgery (doctor's office)?	의사는 어디에 있읍니까?	ŭi·sa·nŭn ŏ·di·e i·ssŭm·ni·ka
What are the surgery (office) hours?	진료 시간은 몇시부터 몇시까지입니까?	chil·lyo shi·gan·ŭn myŏt·shi·bu·t'ŏ myŏt·shi·ka·ji·im·ni·ka
Could the doctor come and see me here?	의사가 여기까지 왕진해 줄까요?	ŭi·sa·ga yŏ·gi·ka·ji wang·jin·hae chul·ka·yo
What time can the doctor come?	의사는 몇시에 올 수 있을까요?	ŭi·sa·nŭn myŏt·shi·e ol·su i·ssŭl·ka·yo

Symptoms

Use this section to tell the doctor what is wrong. Basically, what he'll require to know is:

What? (ache, pain, bruise, etc.)
Where? (arm, stomach, etc.)
How long? (have you had the trouble)

Before you visit the doctor find out the answers to these questions by glancing through the pages that follow. In this way you'll save time.

Parts of the body

ankle	발목	pal·mok
appendix	맹장	maeng·jang
arm	팔	p'al
artery	동맥	tong·maek
back	등	tŭng
bladder	방광	pang·gwang
blood	피	p'i
bone	뼈	pyŏ
bowels	장	chang
breast	유방	yu·bang

DOCTOR

chest	가슴	ka·sŭm
collar-bone	쇄골	swe·gol
ear	귀	kwi
elbow	팔꿈치	p'al·kum·ch'i
eye	눈	nun
face	얼굴	ŏl·gul
finger	손가락	son·ka·rak
foot	발	pal
gland	선	sŏn
hand	손	son
head	머리	mŏ·ri
heart	심장	shim·jang
heel	뒤꿈치	twi·kum·ch'i
hip	엉덩이	ŏng·dŏng·i
intestines	장	chang
jaw	턱	t'ŏk
joint	관절	kwan·jŏl
kidney	신장	shin·jang
knee	무릎	mu·rŭp
leg	다리	ta·ri
liver	간장	kan·jang
lung	폐	p'ye
mouth	입	ip
muscle	근육	kŭn·yuk
neck	목	mok
nerve	신경	shin·gyŏng
nervous system	신경계통	shin·gyŏng kye·t'ong
nose	코	k'o
rib	늑골	nŭk·kol
shoulder	어깨	ŏ·kae
skin	피부	p'i·bu
spine	척추	ch'ŏk·ch'u
stomach	위	wi
tendon	전	kŏn
thigh	넓적다리	nŏp·chŏk·ta·ri
throat	목구멍	mok·ku·mŏng
thumb	엄지손가락	ŏm·ji·son·ga·rak
toe	발가락	pal·ga·rak
tongue	혀	hyŏ
tonsils	편도선	p'yŏn·do·sŏn
urine	오줌	o·jum
vein	정맥	chŏng·maek
wrist	손목	son·mok

PATIENT

Part 1—Illness

I'm not feeling well.	몸이 불편합니다.	mom·i pul·p'yŏn·ham·ni·da
I'm ill.	몸이 아픕니다.	mom·i a·p'ŭm·ni·da
I've got a pain here.	여기가 아픕니다.	yŏ·gi·ga a·p'ŭm·ni·da
His/Her . . . hurts.	그/그녀는 …이 아픕니다.	kŭ/kŭ·nyŏ·nŭn . . . i a·p'ŭm·ni·da
I've got a . . .	나는 …이 아픕니다.	na·nŭn . . . i a·p'ŭm·ni·da
headache/back-ache/sore throat	머리/등/목구멍	mŏ·ri/tŭng/mok·ku·mŏng
I'm constipated.	변비증에 걸렸읍니다.	pyŏn·bi·jŭng·e kŏl·lyŏ·ssŭm·ni·da
I've been vomiting.	구토증이 납니다.	ku·t'o·jŭng·i nam·ni·da

DOCTOR

제 1 부—증상

무슨 일이죠?	What's the trouble?
어디가 아프십니까?	Where does it hurt?
아픈 지 얼마나 되었읍니까?	How long have you had this pain?
이런 상태가 얼마나 계속되었읍니까?	How long have you been feeling like this?
소매를 걷어 올리세요.	Roll up your sleeve.
웃도리를 벗어 주세요.	Please undress down to the waist.
바지와 팬츠를 벗어 주세요.	Please remove your trousers and underpants.

DOCTOR

PATIENT

I feel . . .	저는…	chŏ·nŭn . . .
ill/sick	몸이 불편합니다.	mom·i pul·p'yŏn·ham·ni·da
faint/dizzy	정신이 몽롱합니다/현기 증이 납니다.	chŏng·shin·i mong·nong· ham·ni·da/hyŏn·gi·jŭng·i nam·ni·da
nauseous/shivery	구토증이 납니다/오한이 납니다.	ku·t'o·jŭng·i nam·ni·da/o· han·i nam·ni·da
I/He/She's got (a/an) . . .	저는/그는/그녀는…	chŏ·nŭn/kŭ·nŭn/ kŭ·nyŏ·nŭn . . .
abscess	종기가 났읍니다.	chong·gi·ga na·ssŭm·ni·da
asthma	천식에 걸렸읍니다.	ch'ŏn·shi·ge kŏl·lyŏ·ssŭm· ni·da
chill	오한이 납니다.	o·han·i nam·ni·da
cold	감기에 걸렸읍니다.	kam·gi·e kŏl·lyŏ·ssŭm·ni·da
constipation	변비에 걸렸읍니다.	pyŏn·bi·e kŏl·lyŏ·ssŭm·ni·da
convulsions	경련이 납니다.	kyŏng·nyŏn·i nam·ni·da
cramps	쥐가 났읍니다.	chwi·ga na·ssŭm·ni·da
diarrhoea	설사가 납니다.	sŏl·sa·ga nam·ni·da
fever	열이 납니다.	yŏ·ri nam·ni·da
haemorrhoids	치질에 걸렸읍니다.	ch'i·ji·re kŏl·lyŏ·ssŭm·ni·da

DOCTOR

여기 누워 주세요.	Please lie down over here.
입을 벌리세요.	Open your mouth.
심호흡하세요.	Breathe deeply.
기침을 해봐 주세요.	Cough, please.
체온을 재어 봅시다.	I'll take your temperature.
혈압을 재겠읍니다.	I'm going to take your blood pressure.
이런 증상은 처음입니까?	Is this the first time .you've had this?
주사를 놓겠읍니다.	I'll give you an injection.
소변을/대변을 검사해 봐야겠읍니다.	I want a specimen of your urine/stools.

PATIENT

hernia	탈장이 됐읍니다.	t'al·chang·i twe·ssŭm·ni·da
indigestion	소화불량입니다.	so·hwa·bul·lyang·im·ni·da
inflammation of ...	...에 염증이 있읍니다.	... e yŏm·jŭng·i i·ssŭm·ni·da
influenza	독감입니다.	tok·kam·im·ni·da
morning sickness	입덧을 합니다.	ip·tŏ·sŭl ham·ni·da
stiff neck	목이 뻣뻣합니다.	mo·gi pŏt·pŏt·ham·ni·da
rheumatism	류마티스에 걸렸읍니다.	ryu·ma·t'i·sŭ·e kŏl·lyŏ·ssŭm·ni·da
sunburn	햇볕에 탔읍니다.	haet·byŏ't'e t'a·ssŭm·ni·da
sunstroke	일사병에 걸렸읍니다.	il·sa·byŏng·e kŏl·lyŏ·ssŭm·ni·da
tonsillitis	편도선염입니다.	p'yŏn·do·sŏn·yŏm·im·ni·da
ulcer	궤양입니다.	kwe·yang·im·ni·da
It's nothing serious, I hope.	대단치는 않을 겁니다.	tae·dan·ch'i·nŭn a·nŭl kŏm·ni·da
I'd like you to prescribe me some medicine.	약 좀 처방해 주셨으면 하는데요.	yak chom ch'ŏ·bang·hae chu·syŏ·ssŭ·myŏn ha·nŭn·de·yo

DOCTOR

DOCTOR

걱정할 것은 없읍니다.	It's nothing to worry about.
...일간 안정하셔야 합니다.	You must stay in bed for ... days.
당신은...	You've got ...
감기에 걸렸군요/관절염입니다/폐렴입니다/독감에 걸렸군요/식중독에 걸렸군요/...에 염증이 생겼어요.	a cold/arthritis/pneumonia/influenza/food poisoning/an inflammation of ...
담배를 너무 피우시는군요/술을 너무 마시는군요.	You're smoking/drinking too much.
과로입니다. 쉬셔야겠어요.	You're over-tired. You need a rest.
전문의의 진찰을 받으시지요.	I want you to see a specialist.
병원에 가셔서 종합 진찰을 받으시지요.	I want you to go to the hospital for a general check-up.
항생 물질을 처방하지요.	I'll prescribe an antibiotic.

PATIENT

I'm a diabetic.	저는 당뇨병에 걸렸읍니다.	chŏ·nŭn tang·nyo·byŏng·e kŏl·lyŏ·ssŭm·ni·da
I've a cardiac condition.	저는 심장병 기미가 있읍니다.	chŏ·nŭn shim·jang·byŏng ki·mi·ga i·ssŭm·ni·da
I had a heart attack in ...	...에 심장 발작이 있었읍니다.	...e shim·jang pal·cha·gi i·ssŏ·ssŭm·ni·da
I'm allergic to ...	...에 대해 알레르기 증상이 있읍니다.	...e tae·hae al·le·rŭ·gi chŭng·sang·i i·ssŭm·ni·da
This is my usual medicine.	이것이 제가 상복하는 약입니다.	i·gŏ·shi che·ga sang·bok·ha·nŭn ya·gim·ni·da
I need this medicine.	이 약을 원하는데요.	i ya·gŭl wŏn·ha·nŭn·de·yo
I'm expecting a baby. Can I travel?	저는 임신했는데요, 여행해도 괜찮을까요?	chŏ·nŭn im·shin·haen·nŭn·de·yo, yŏ·haeng·hae·do kwen·ch'an·ŭl·ka·yo

DOCTOR

인슐린의 한 번 복용량은 얼마나 됩니까?	What dose of insulin are you taking?
주사입니까, 또는 내복약입니까?	Injection or oral?
무슨 치료를 받아 오고 있읍니까?	What treatment have you been having?
무슨 약을 복용해 오고 있읍니까?	What medicine have you been taking?
(가벼운) 심장 발작입니다.	You've had a (slight) heart attack.
한국에서는 ...은 사용하고 있지 않습니다. 이것은 아주 비슷한 약입니다.	We don't use... in Korea. This is very similar.
출산 예정일이 언제입니까?	When is the baby due?
...까지는 여행해서는 안됩니다.	You can't travel until ...

PATIENT

Part 2—Wounds

Could you have a look at this . . . ?	이 …을 보아 주시겠어요?	i . . . ŭl po·a chu·shi·ge·ssŏ·yo
blister	물집	mul·chip
boil	종기	chong·gi
bruise	타박상	t'a·bak·sang
burn	화상	hwa·sang
cut	베인 상처	pe·in sang·ch'ŏ
graze	찰과상	ch'al·gwa·sang
insect bite	벌레 물린 데	pŏl·le mul·lin te
lump	혹	hok
rash	발진	pal·chin
sting	찔린 상처	chil·lin sang·ch'ŏ
swelling	종기	chong·gi
wound	상처	sang·ch'ŏ
I can't move my . . . It hurts.	…이 아파서 움직일 수가 없는데요.	. . . i a·p'a·sŏ um·ji·gil·su·ga ŏm·nŭn·de·yo

DOCTOR

제 2 부—상처

화농했읍니다(하지 않았읍니다).	It's (not) infected.
탈구했읍니다.	You've got a slipped disc.
엑스레이를 찍으셔야겠읍니다.	I want you to have an X-ray.
…되어 있읍니다.	It's . . .
부러진／삔	broken/sprained
탈구된／찢긴	dislocated/torn
근육을 너무 당기셨군요.	You've pulled a muscle.
항생제를 드리지요.	I'll give you an antiseptic.
대단치는 않습니다.	It's not serious.
…일 지난 뒤에 다시 한번 오시기 바랍니다.	I want you to come and see me in . . . days' time.

PATIENT

Part 3—Nervous tension

I'm in a nervous state.	신경과민 상태에 있읍니다.	shin·gyŏng·gwa·min sang·t'ae·e i·ssŭm·ni·da
I'm feeling depressed.	기분이 우울합니다.	ki·bun·i u·ul·ham·ni·da
I want some sleeping pills.	수면제를 좀 주셨으면 하는데요.	su·myŏn·je·rŭl chom chu·syŏ·ssŭ·myŏn ha·nŭn·de·yo
I can't eat/sleep.	식욕이 없읍니다/잠이 잘 오지 않습니다.	shi·gyo·gi ŏp·sŭm·ni·da/cham·i chal o·ji an·sŭm·ni·da
I'm having night-mares.	가위 눌리는 일이 많습니다.	ka·wi·nul·li·nŭn i·ri man·sŭm·ni·da
Can you prescribe a...?	…을 처방해 주시겠어요?	...ŭl ch'ŏ·bang·hae chu·shi·ge·ssŏ·yo
sedative	진정제	chin·jŏng·je
tranquilizer	진정제	chin·jŏng·je
anti-depressant	항울제	hang·ul·che

DOCTOR

제 3 부—신경과민증

신경과민증에 걸리셨군요.	You're suffering from nervous tension.
안정이 필요합니다.	You need a rest.
무슨 약을 쓰고 계십니까?	What pills have you been taking?
하루에 몇 정입니까?	How many a day?
이런 증상이 일어난 지 얼마나 되었읍니까?	How long have you been feeling like this?
약을 좀 처방해 드리지요.	I'll prescribe some pills.
진정제를 드리지요.	I'll give you a sedative.

DOCTOR

PATIENT

Prescriptions and dosage

What kind of medicine is this?	이것은 무슨 약입니까?	i·gŏ·sŭn mu·sŭn ya·gim·ni·ka
How many times a day should I take it?	하루에 몇 번 복용해야 합니까?	ha·ru·e myŏt·bŏn po·gyong·hae·ya ham·ni·ka
Must I swallow them whole?	모두 한꺼번에 삼켜야 합니까?	mo·du han·kŏ·bŏn·e sam·k'yŏ·ya ham·ni·ka

Fee

How much do I owe you?	얼맘니까?	ŏl·mam·ni·ka
Do I pay you now or will you send me your bill?	지금 지불할까요, 그렇지 않으면 청구서를 보내 주시겠어요?	chi·gŭm chi·bul·hal·ka·yo, kŭ·rŏ·ch'i a·nŭ·myŏn ch'ŏng·gu·sŏ·rŭl po·nae chu·shi·ge·ssŏ·yo
Thanks for your help, doctor.	선생님, 여러 가지로 감사합니다.	sŏn·saeng·nim, yŏ·rŏ·ga·ji·ro kam·sa·ham·ni·da

DOCTOR

약의 처방

이 약을 …시간마다 …스푼씩 복용하세요.	Take ... teaspoons of this medicine every ... hours.
…정을 물 한 컵으로 복용하세요.	Take ... tablets with a glass of water.
하루에 …번	... times a day
식사 전에	before each meal
식후에	after each meal
아침에	in the mornings
밤에	at night

치료비

천원입니다.	That's 1000 won, please.
지금 지불해 주세요.	Please pay me now.
청구서를 보내 드리겠읍니다.	I'll send you a bill.

Dentist

Can you recommend a good dentist?	잘 하는 치과 의사를 소개해 주시겠어요?	chal ha·nŭn ch'i·kwa ŭi·sa·rŭl so·gae·hae chu·shi·ge·ssŏ·yo
Can I make an (urgent) appointment to see Doctor . . . ?	(급히) …선생님의 진찰을 받을 수 없을까요?	(kŭ·p'i) . . . sŏn·saeng·nim·ŭi chin·ch'a·rŭl pa·dŭl·su ŏp·sŭl·ka·yo
Can't you possibly make it earlier than that?	더 빨리 해주실 수 없을까요?	tŏ pal·li hae·ju·shil·su ŏp·sŭl·ka·yo
I've a toothache.	이가 아픕니다.	i·ga a·p'ŭm·ni·da
I've an abscess.	종기가 났습니다.	chong·gi·ga na·ssŭm·ni·da
This tooth hurts.	이 이가 아픕니다.	i i·ga a·p'ŭm·ni·da
at the top	위입니다.	wi·im·ni·da
at the bottom	아래입니다.	a·rae·im·ni·da
in the front	앞입니다.	a·p'im·ni·da
at the back	안쪽입니다.	an·chok·im·ni·da
Can you fix it temporarily ?	응급 조치를 해주실 수 있습니까?	ŭng·gŭp cho·ch'i·rŭl hae·ju·shil·su i·ssŭm·ni·ka
I don't want it extracted (pulled).	빼지 말고 해주셨으면 좋겠습니다.	pae·ji mal·go hae·ju·syŏ·ssŭ·myŏn cho·k'e·ssŭm·ni·da
I've lost a filling.	충전한 것이 없어졌어요.	ch'ung·jŏn·han kŏ·shi ŏp·sŏ·jŏ·ssŏ·yo
The gum is very sore/ The gum is bleeding.	잇몸이 몹시 아픕니다/ 잇몸에 피가 납니다.	in·mom·i mop·shi a·p'ŭm·ni·da/in·mom·e p'i·ga nam·ni·da

Dentures

I've broken this denture.	의치가 깨졌는데요.	ŭi·ch'i·ga kae·jŏn·nŭn·de·yo
Can you repair this denture?	이 의치를 고칠 수 있습니까?	i ŭi·ch'i·rŭl ko·ch'il·su i·ssŭm·ni·ka
When will it be ready?	언제 될까요?	ŏn·je toel·ka·yo

Optician

I've broken my glasses.	안경이 깨졌는데요.	an·gyŏng·i kae·jŏn·nŭn·de·yo
Can you repair them for me?	고쳐 주실 수 있겠읍니까?	ko·ch'ŏ chu·shil·su i·ke·ssŭm·ni·ka
When will they be ready?	언제 될까요?	ŏn·je toel·ka·yo
Can you change the lenses?	렌즈를 바꿀 수 있읍니까?	len·jŭ·rŭl pa·kul·su i·ssŭm·ni·ka
I want some contact lenses.	콘택트 렌즈를 해 넣으려고 하는데요.	k'on·t'aek·t'ŭ len·jŭ·rŭl hae·nŏ·ŭ·ryŏ·go ha·nŭn·de·yo
I want tinted lenses.	색깔이 있는 렌즈를 원합니다.	sae·ka·ri in·nŭn len·jŭ·rŭl wŏn·ham·ni·da
I'd like to buy a pair of binoculars.	쌍안경을 하나 사려고 하는데요.	ssang·an·gyŏng·ŭl ha·na sa·ryŏ·go ha·nŭn·de·yo
How much do I owe you?	얼맙니까?	ŏl·mam·ni·ka
Do I pay you now or will you send me your bill?	지금 지불해 드릴까요, 그렇지 않으면 청구서를 보내 주시겠읍니까?	chi·gŭm chi·bul·hae tŭ·ril·ka·yo, kŭ·rŏ·ch'i a·nŭ·myŏn ch'ŏng·gu·sŏ·rŭl po·nae chu·shi·ge·ssŭm·ni·ka

OPTICIAN

FOR NUMBERS, see page 175

Reference section

Where do you come from?

This page will help you to explain where you're from, where you've been or where you're going.

Africa	아프리카	a·p'ŭ·ri·k'a
Asia	아시아	a·shi·a
Australia	오스트레일리아	o·sŭ·t'ŭ·re·il·li·a
Belgium	벨기에	bel·gi·e
Burma	버마	bŏ·ma
Canada	캐나다	k'ae·na·da
China	중국	chung·guk
Denmark	덴마크	den·ma·k'ŭ
Europe	유럽	yu·rŏp
Finland	핀란드	p'il·lan·dŭ
France	프랑스	p'ŭ·rang·sŭ
Germany	독일	to·gil
Great Britain	영국	yŏng·guk
India	인도	in·do
Indonesia	인도네시아	in·do·ne·shi·a
Ireland	아일랜드	a·il·lan·dŭ
Italy	이탈리아	i·t'al·li·a
Japan	일본	il·bon
Korea	한국	han·guk
Malaysia	말레이지아	mal·le·i·ji·a
Netherlands	네델란드	ne·del·lan·dŭ
New Zealand	뉴질랜드	nyu·jil·laen·dŭ
North America	북미	pung·mi
Norway	노르웨이	no·rŭ·we·i
Philippines	필리핀	p'il·li·p'in
South Africa	남아프리카	nam·a·p'ŭ·ri·k'a
South America	남미	nam·mi
Sweden	스웨덴	sŭ·we·den
Switzerland	스위스	sŭ·wi·sŭ
Taiwan	대만	tae·man
Thailand	태국	t'ae·guk
USA	미국	mi·guk

Numbers

0	영	yŏng
1	일/하나	il/hana
2	이/둘	i/tul
3	삼/셋	sam/set
4	사/넷	sa/net
5	오/다섯	o/ta·sŏt
6	육/여섯	yuk/yŏ·sŏt
7	칠/일곱	ch'il/il·gop
8	팔/여덟	p'al/yŏ·dŏl
9	구/아홉	ku/a·hop
10	십/열	ship/yŏl
11	십일	shi·bil
12	십이	shi·bi
13	십삼	ship·sam
14	십사	ship·sa
15	십오	shi·bo
16	십육	shim·nyuk
17	십칠	ship·ch'il
18	십팔	shi·p'al
19	십구	ship·ku
20	이십	i·ship
21	이십일	i·shi·bil
22	이십이	i·shi·bi
23	이십삼	i·ship·sam
24	이십사	i·ship·sa
25	이십오	i·shi·bo
26	이십육	i·shim·nyuk
27	이십칠	i·ship·ch'il
28	이십팔	i·shi·p'al
29	이십구	i·ship·ku
30	삼십	sam·ship
31	삼십일	sam·shi·bil
32	삼십이	sam·shi·bi
33	삼십삼	sam·ship·sam
40	사십	sa·ship
41	사십일	sa·shi·bil
42	사십이	sa·shi·bi
43	사십삼	sa·ship·sam
50	오십	o·ship
51	오십일	o·shi·bil
52	오십이	o·shi·bi
53	오십삼	o·ship·sam

60	육십	yuk·ship
61	육십일	yuk·shi·bil
62	육십이	yuk·shi·bi
70	칠십	ch'il·ship
71	칠십일	ch'il·shi·bil
72	칠십이	ch'il·shi·bi
80	팔십	p'al·ship
81	팔십일	p'al·shi·bil
82	팔십이	p'al·shi·bi
90	구십	ku·ship
91	구십일	ku·shi·bil
92	구십이	ku·shi·bi
100	백	paek
101	백일	pae·gil
102	백이	pae·gi
110	백십	paek·ship
120	백이십	pae·gi·ship
130	백삼십	paek·sam·ship
140	백사십	paek·sa·ship
150	백오십	pae·go·ship
160	백육십	paeng·nyuk·ship
170	백칠십	paek·ch'il·ship
180	백팔십	paek·p'al·ship
190	백구십	paek·ku·ship
200	이백	i·baek
300	삼백	sam·baek
400	사백	sa·baek
500	오백	o·baek
600	육백	yuk·paek
700	칠백	ch'il·baek
800	팔백	p'al·baek
900	구백	ku·baek
1000	천	ch'ŏn
1100	천백	ch'ŏn·baek
1200	천이백	ch'ŏn·i·baek
2000	이천	i·ch'ŏn
5000	오천	o·ch'ŏn
10,000	만	man
50,000	오만	o·man
100,000	십만	shim·man
1,000,000	백만	paeng·man
1,000,000,000	십억	shi·bŏk

first	첫째	ch'ŏt·chae
second	둘째	tul·chae
third	세째	se·chae
fourth	네째	ne·chae
fifth	다섯째	ta·sŏt·chae
sixth	여섯째	yŏ·sŏt·chae
seventh	일곱째	il·gop·chae
eighth	여덟째	yŏ·dŏl·chae
ninth	아홉째	a·hop·chae
tenth	열째	yŏl·chae
once	한번	han·bŏn
twice	두번	tu·bŏn
three times	세번	se·bŏn
a half	반	pan
half a ...	...의 반	... ŭi pan
half of ...	...의 반	... ŭi pan
half (adj.)	반의	pan·ŭi
a quarter	사분의 일	sa·bun·ŭi il
one third	삼분의 일	sam·bun·ŭi il
a pair of	한 벌의	han pŏl·ŭi
a dozen	한 타스	han t'a·sŭ
1981	천구백팔십일	ch'ŏn·gu·baek·p'al·shi·bil
1992	천구백구십이	ch'ŏn·gu·baek·gu·shi·bi
2003	이천삼	i·ch'ŏn·sam

Note: In Korean, cardinal numbers are pronounced in two different ways though they are both written with the same Arabic numeral. So, for example, **il** or **hana** may be used for saying the number one, and **sam** or **set** for three. It is recommended, however, that you use **hana** for one and **set** for three in conversation.

REFERENCE SECTION

Time

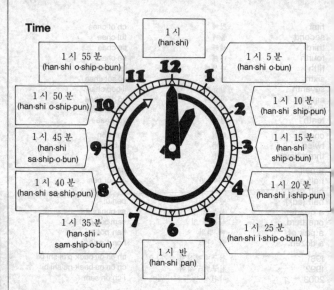

1 시
(han·shi)

1 시 55 분
(han·shi o·ship·o·bun)

1 시 5 분
(han·shi o·bun)

1 시 50 분
(han·shi o·ship·pun)

1 시 10 분
(han·shi ship·pun)

1 시 45 분
(han·shi sa·ship·o·bun)

1 시 15 분
(han·shi ship·o·bun)

1 시 40 분
(han·shi sa·ship·pun)

1 시 20 분
(han·shi i·ship·pun)

1 시 35 분
(han·shi sam·ship·o·bun)

1 시 25 분
(han·shi i·ship·o·bun)

1 시 반
(han·shi pan)

What time is it ?	지금 몇시입니까 ?	chi·gŭm myŏt·shi·im·ni·ka
Excuse me. Can you tell me the time ?	미안하지만 지금 몇시입니까 ?	mi·an·ha·ji·man chi·gŭm myŏt·shi·im·ni·ka
I'll meet you at ... tomorrow.	내일 ...시에 뵙지요.	nae·il ... shi·e poep·chi·yo
I'm so sorry I'm late.	늦어서 대단히 미안합니다.	nŭ·jŏ·sŏ tae·dan·hi mi·an·ham·ni·da
after	후	hu
before	전	chŏn
early	일찌기	il·chi·gi
in time	제시간에	che·shi·gan·e
late	늦은	nŭ·jŭn
midday (noon)	정오	chŏng·o
midnight	자정	cha·jŏng

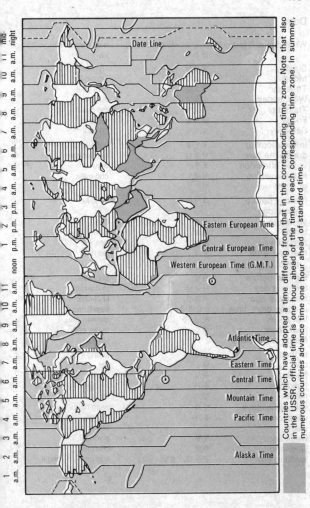

Countries which have adopted a time differing from that in the corresponding time zone. Note that also in the USSR, official time is one hour ahead of the time in each corresponding time zone. In summer, numerous countries advance time one hour ahead of standard time.

Date Line

Eastern European Time
Central European Time
Western European Time (G.M.T.)

Atlantic Time
Eastern Time
Central Time
Mountain Time
Pacific Time
Alaska Time

1 a.m. 2 a.m. 3 a.m. 4 a.m. 5 a.m. 6 a.m. 7 a.m. 8 a.m. 9 a.m. 10 a.m. 11 a.m. noon p.m. 1 p.m. 2 p.m. 3 a.m. 4 a.m. 5 a.m. 6 a.m. 7 a.m. 8 a.m. 9 a.m. 10 a.m. 11 a.m. mid-night

Days

What day is it today ?	오늘은 무슨 요일입니까 ?	o·nŭ·rŭn mu·sŭn yo·il·im·ni·ka
Sunday	일요일	i·ryo·il
Monday	월요일	wŏ·ryo·il
Tuesday	화요일	hwa·yo·il
Wednesday	수요일	su·yo·il
Thursday	목요일	mo·gyo·il
Friday	금요일	kŭ·myo·il
Saturday	토요일	t'o·yo·il
in the morning	오전중	o·jŏn·jung
during the day	낮동안	nat·dong·an
in the afternoon	오후	o·hu
in the evening	저녁	chŏ·nyŏk
at night	밤	pam
the day before yesterday	그저께	kŭ·jŏ·ke
yesterday	어제	ŏ·je
today	오늘	o·nŭl
tomorrow	내일	nae·il
the day after tomorrow	모레	mo·rae
the day before	전날	chŏn·nal
the next day	다음날	ta·ŭm·nal
two days ago	이틀전	i·t'ŭl·chŏn
in three days' time	3 일내에	sam·il·nae·e
last week	지난 주	chi·nan chu
next week	다음 주	ta·ŭm chu
during two weeks	2 주간	i·ju·gan
birthday	생일	saeng·il
day	날	nal
holiday	휴일	hyu·il
holidays	휴가	hyu·ga
month	달	tal
school holidays	방학	pang·hak
vacation	휴가	hyu·ga
week	주	chu
weekday	평일	p'yŏng·il
weekend	주말	chu·mal
working day	근무일, 평일	kŭn·mu·il, p'yŏng·il

Months

The official Korean calendar virtually corresponds to our Gregorian calendar. However, traditional holidays are still celebrated in accordance with the lunar, or Chinese calendar. People in rural farming and fishing communities adhere more closely to the lunar calendar, as has been the practice for a long time. As a result, two New Years are celebrated in Korea: The official one on January 1st, which is a three-day holiday, and the lunar New Year, which usually falls sometime in February.

In Korean, months are literally called first month, second month, third month, etc., which corresponds to our January, February, March, etc. For the convenience of Occidental travellers, however, the days and dates are sure to be written in Western style.

January	1월	i·rwŏl
February	2월	i·wŏl
March	3월	sam·wŏl
April	4월	sa·wŏl
May	5월	o·wŏl
June	6월	yu·wŏl
July	7월	ch'i·rwŏl
August	8월	p'a·rwŏl
September	9월	ku·wŏl
October	10월	shi·wŏl
November	11월	shi·bi·rwŏl
December	12월	shi·bi·wŏl
since June	6월부터	yu·wŏl·bu·t'ŏ
during the month of August	8월 동안	p'a·rwŏl tong·an
last month	지난달	chi·nan·dal
next month	내달	nae·dal
the month before	그 전달	kŭ chŏn·dal
the next month	그 다음달	kŭ ta·ŭm·dal
July 1	7월 1일	ch'i·rwŏl i·ril
March 17	3월 17일	sam·wŏl ship·ch'i·ril

Letter headings are written thus:

Seoul, August 17, 1986	서울에서, 1986년 8월 17일
Pusan, July 1, 1986	부산에서, 1986년 7월 1일

REFERENCE SECTION

Seasons

spring	봄	pom
summer	여름	yŏ·rŭm
autumn	가을	ka·ŭl
winter	겨울	kyŏ·ul
in spring	봄에	po·me
during the summer	여름 동안	yŏ·rŭm tong·an
in autumn	가을에	ka·ŭ·re
during the winter	겨울 동안	kyŏ·ul tong·an

Public holidays

The following list isn't complete. We have noted only the most important public holidays celebrated in Korea. On most of these, banks, offices, shops and stores are closed.

January 1	New Year's Day
March 1	Anniversary of Independence Movement
May 5	Children's Day
June 6	Memorial Day
July 17	Constitution Day
August 15	Liberation Day
October 3	National Foundation Day
December 25	Christmas

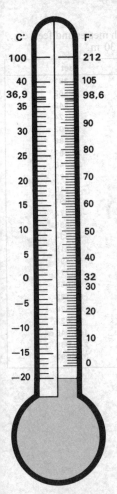

Conversion tables

To change centimetres into inches, multiply by .39.

To change inches into centimetres, multiply by 2.54.

Centimetres and inches

	in.	feet	yards
1 mm	0,039	0,003	0,001
1 cm	0,39	0,03	0,01
1 dm	3,94	0,32	0,10
1 m	39,40	3,28	1,09

	mm	cm	m
1 in.	25,4	2,54	0,025
1 ft.	304,8	30,48	0,304
1 yd.	914,4	91,44	0,914

(32 metres = 35 yards)

Temperature

To convert Centigrade into degrees Fahrenheit, multiply Centigrade by 1.8 and add 32.

To convert degrees Fahrenheit into Centigrade, subtract 32 from Fahrenheit and divide by 1.8.

Metres and feet

The figure in the middle stands for both metres and feet, e.g.,
1 metre = 3,281 ft. and 1 foot = 0,30 m.

Metres		Feet
0.30	1	3.281
0.61	2	6.563
0.91	3	9.843
1.22	4	13.124
1.52	5	16.403
1.83	6	19.686
2.13	7	22.967
2.44	8	26.248
2.74	9	29.529
3.05	10	32.810
3.35	11	36.091
3.66	12	39.372
3.96	13	42.635
4.27	14	45.934
4.57	15	49.215
4.88	16	52.496
5.18	17	55.777
5.49	18	59.058
5.79	19	62.339
6.10	20	65.620
7.62	25	82.023
15.24	50	164.046
22.86	75	246.069
30.48	100	328.092

Other conversion charts

Weight conversion

The figure in the middle stands for both kilograms and pounds, e.g., 1 kilogram = 2.205 lb. and 1 pound = 0.45 kilograms.

Kilograms (kg.)		Avoirdupois pounds
0.45	1	2.205
0.90	2	4.405
1.35	3	6.614
1.80	4	8.818
2.25	5	11.023
2.70	6	13.227
3.15	7	15.432
3.60	8	17.636
4.05	9	19.840
4.50	10	22.045
6.75	15	33.068
9.00	20	44.889
11.25	25	55.113
22.50	50	110.225
33.75	75	165.338
45.00	100	220.450

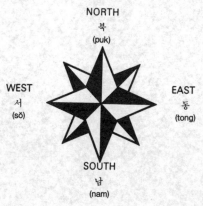

NORTH
북
(puk)

WEST
서
(sŏ)

EAST
동
(tong)

SOUTH
남
(nam)

The year round...

Here are the average temperatures for some Korean cities (in degrees Centigrade).

	Seoul	Pusan	Taegu	Taejon	Kwangju
January	-3.5	2.2	-0.9	-2.1	-0.2
February	-1.1	3.8	1.2	-0.3	1.4
March	4.1	7.7	6.2	4.3	5.8
April	11.4	12.7	12.6	11.9	12.3
May	17.1	17.1	18.1	17.1	17.5
June	21.1	20.0	21.9	21.4	21.5
July	24.5	23.9	25.6	24.9	25.5
August	25.3	25.5	26.1	25.1	26.2
September	20.5	21.8	20.8	20.1	21.2
October	13.9	17.0	14.8	13.3	14.9
November	6.6	11.1	8.0	6.1	8.5
December	-0.6	5.1	1.7	-0.2	2.6

What does that sign mean?

You may encounter some of the following signs or notices on your trip through Korea:

개조심	Beware of the dog
경고	Warning
금연	No smoking
…금지	… forbidden
낚시금지	No fishing
남자용	Gentlemen
노크하지 말고 들어오세요	Enter without knocking
닫혔음	Closed
당기시오	Pull
뜨거움	Hot
만지지 마시오	Don't touch
미시오	Push
벨을 눌러 주세요	Please ring
비상구	Emergency exit
비었음	Vacant
사용중	Occupied
사유지	Private property
세 놓습니다	To let (for hire)
안내	Information
엘리베이터	Lift (elevator)
여자용	Ladies
염가 대매출	Sale
예약필	Reserved
위험	Danger
입구	Entrance
입장금지	No entrance
입장사절	No admittance
정지	Stop
주의	Caution
차가움	Cold
출구	Exit
출납계	Cashier's
출입금지	Keep out
치명적 위험	Danger of death
팔 것	For sale
품절	Sold out

REFERENCE SECTION

Emergency !

By the time the emergency is upon you, it's too late to turn to this page to find the Korean for "I'll scream if you ...". So have a look at this short list beforehand—and, if you want to be on the safe side, learn the expressions shown in capitals.

Be quick	빨리 !	pal·li
Call the police	경찰을 불러 주세요.	kyŏng·ch'a·rŭl pul·lŏ chu·se·yo
CAREFUL	주의	chu·ŭi
Come here	이리 오세요.	i·ri o·se·yo
Danger	위험	wi·hŏm
Fire	불	pul
Gas	가스	ga·sŭ
Get a doctor	의사를 불러 주세요.	ŭi·sa·rŭl pul·lŏ chu·se·yo
Go away	가세요 !	ka·se·yo
HELP	사람 살려 !	sa·ram sal·lyŏ
Get help quickly	누구 좀 빨리 불러 주세요.	nu·gu chom pal·li pul·lŏ chu·se·yo
I'm ill	저는 몸이 아픕니다.	chŏ·nŭn mom·i a·p'ŭm·ni·da
I'm lost	길을 잃었어요.	ki·rŭl i·rŏ·ssŏ·yo
I've lost my ...	...을 잃어버렸어요.	...ŭl i·rŏ·bŏ·ryŏ·ssŏ·yo
Leave me alone	상관하지마세요.	sang·gwan·ha·ji ma·se·yo
Lie down	드러 누우세요.	tŭ·rŏ·nu·u·se·yo
Listen	들으세요.	tŭ·rŭ·se·yo
Listen to me	제 말을 들어 보세요.	che ma·rŭl tŭ·rŏ·bo·se·yo
Look	보세요	po·se·yo
LOOK OUT	주위를 잘 살피세요.	chu·wi·rŭl chal sal·p'i·se·yo
POLICE	경찰	kyŏng·ch'al
Stop	정지	chŏng·ji
Stop here	여기서 세우세요.	yŏ·gi·sŏ se·u·se·yo
Stop that man	저 남자를 붙잡아 주세요.	chŏ nam·ja·rŭl put·ja·ba chu·se·yo
STOP THIEF	도둑놈 잡아요 !	to·duk·nom cha·ba·yo
Stop or I'll scream	그만 두지 않으면 소리를 지를 테에요.	kŭ·man tu·ji a·nŭ·myŏn so·ri·rŭl chi·rŭl·t'e·e·yo

FOR CAR ACCIDENTS, see page 149

Emergency numbers

Ambulance ....

Fire ....

Police ....

Fill in these as well

Embassy ....

Consulate ....

Taxi ....

Airport information ....

Travel agent ....

Hotel ....

Restaurant ....

Babysitter ....

....

....

....

....

....

....

....

....

Index